Parks,
People,
Preservation,
and Public Policy

Parks, People, Preservation, and Public Policy

Eleanor Boggs Shoemaker

iUniverse, Inc.
New York   Bloomington

Parks, People, Preservation, and Public Policy

Copyright © 2010 Eleanor Boggs Shoemaker

iUniverse books may be ordered through booksellers or by contacting:

iUniverse
1663 Liberty Drive
Bloomington, IN 47403
www.iuniverse.com
1-800-Authors (1-800-288-4677)

ISBN: 978-1-4502-0235-0 (pbk)
ISBN: 978-1-4502-0237-4 (cloth)
ISBN: 978-1-4502-0236-7 (ebk)

Printed in the United States of America

iUniverse rev. date: 03/25/2010

To Dan and Boggs, my sons, who share with me an abiding love of nature and history and are themselves devoted to preserving places of beauty and meaning for their children. Also, of course, to all of the staff and volunteers who, throughout the years, have created an enviable county park system, I salute you.

Eleanor Boggs Shoemaker

Contents

Preface

The first twenty years of my life were divided between sanguine summers on the Mississippi Gulf Coast and winters at school in Washington DC. It was a study in contrasts: magnificent public buildings filled with history in Washington and the natural wonders of the Mississippi Gulf. Though different in many ways, each place is connected by a common thread. The Gulf Coast and Washington DC are cosmopolitan and transient.

Although I fared well in both places, in 1955, as a bride of twenty, I lost my heart to York County, Pennsylvania. I was captivated by the natural beauty—hills and valleys, the meandering river, carefully cultivated farm fields, the stout-hearted people of the farming community, and the earnest blue-collar workers from the ranks of the diverse manufacturing base. More than anything, the elixir for me was the stability and constancy of the unspoiled countryside and the self-reliant people. I loved the inherent sense of place, the roots. Family was esteemed. People were content, where they wanted to be and had been for generations. York was a community unlike any I had ever known. The pace was steady—seldom idle, yet never frantic. Though not without flaws, York County was the best place to live I could imagine. It still is.

Though I had sailed the Gulf, camped on pine-carpeted forest floors, and biked along the seawall, I had never been to an organized camp. However, with the confidence of youth, soon after arriving in York, I accepted an invitation to direct the YWCA camp, Camp Cannedion. The experience of organized camping captivated me to the extent that in 1967 I organized an affiliate club of the United States Pony Clubs and established a summer camp for children, dedicated to character development via horsemanship at my farm home. The camp continues today under the leadership of my younger son. It was not long before I realized that places like family farms, such as my own, were becoming scarce and, in the future, camps for youth or others would require public sites.

As the years passed, I have had the opportunity to be involved in a myriad of community activities. One of the most gratifying was an association with two men, Harry McLaughlin and Joe Raab, who inspired and encouraged me to lend my energy to the new York County Parks System. They sought to preserve the core attributes of York County for the ages. They recognized the change that was coming. Farms would be absorbed by houses as the county of York entered a period of rapid development. They did not oppose growth, but they were serious advocates of preservation. I responded to their call, and my tenure on the Parks Board exposed me to a well-oiled system strengthening my belief that good planning and good public policy are effective instruments to preserve community characteristics that equal good living. Sufficient evidence exists of unplanned growth throughout our country to affirm a truth: prudent planning and conservation are essential for the maintenance of a good quality of life.

Today, York County is benefiting from the efforts of hundreds of dedicated volunteers and staff, who have successfully saved unspoiled space for the present and the future by employing plans with carefully enunciated guidelines. There is now sufficient public space available in York County to meet the needs for open space well into the future. The York County Department of Parks and Recreation is a success story that I have been privileged to witness. While many communities experience drastic changes that corrode cohesiveness and stability, York County has found ways to retain its natural beauty, stability, and sense of place during a period of rapid change. If, in the future, the well-established, successful policies of York County Parks remain unimpeded, the department will continue to secure the roots of the county—the basis of all stable communities. If there is a caveat, it is that spooning redundant layers of government over effective local agencies is inefficient and costly. In an age of cynicism, public mismanagement, corruption, and scandal, it warms my heart to share this story of local government at its best.

Eleanor Boggs Shoemaker
2009

Acknowledgments

Luther Sowers is a precise editor and a champion of the English language. His oversight has enhanced this book, and I am forever grateful to him for the countless hours he has labored on behalf of readers.

It is because of the astute book committee of the York County Parks that this record will reach the public. I appreciate the insight and direction they have shared. If this story is well told, they have had a large hand in its success.

Chapter 1
Public Parks and Public Policy

o o o o o o o o o o o o o o o o o o o o o o o o o o o o o o o o o

The salutary influence of example.

Samuel Johnson
(1709–1784)

Seeds

This is a brief account of the York County Pennsylvania Parks Department. Its evolution is instructive because as more local governments implement policies to provide for public recreation and land preservation they face the inevitable challenges of balancing public and private interest in an ever-changing world. This story is well worth telling because it is a success story predicated on ideals—ideals considered, cultivated, and realized.

Seeds of public policy germinate in countless ways. Cultivating an idea into a viable policy is usually the result of deliberate planning; but sometimes, good public policy is an unintended consequence, sprouting from other policies, thus, preceding planning.

Whatever the genesis of a policy, convergence of a number of seemingly obvious steps must occur for it to be implemented, evolve, and thrive. The essential criteria for the establishment of successful public policies are recognizable and can be summarized in six sentences:

Criteria for Successful Public Policy

1. A public need must be recognized.
2. A plan to meet the need must be developed.
3. A source of funding must be available.
4. A dynamic leader or team must advocate the benefits.

5. A positive public response must be elicited.
6. An administrative or legislative mandate must vest authority for implementation of the policy in accountable, competent, dedicated hands in a timely way.

Lacking any of the foregoing six ingredients, successful implementation of an enduring public policy is slim.

Trails leading to public policy are often unguided and even more often unexplored. This account tracks the emergence of a successful public policy. It recounts a circuitous history culminating in a public policy establishing the York County (Pennsylvania) Parks System. The story is a microcosm of democracy in action in the United States.

Roots

The challenge facing eighteenth-century forefathers of America was to provide protection for the property rights of individuals. Their hard-fought struggles secured those rights. Though never to be taken for granted, individual property rights are in place, guaranteed by the United States Constitution. Ironically, the challenges confronting citizens of the twentieth century were quite the opposite. Public rights became the focus of policy makers. It was a new time dedicated to securing and protecting public rights to water, open space, air, and links to the past. Public rights became increasingly salient, competing with private rights in new ways. Growing awareness of the shift from an agrarian to an urban society focused attention on securing public spaces where individuals could seek the benefits of connections with nature and its restorative effects on body, mind, and spirit. But such aims must balance public needs and private rights. It is a delicate balance, and it has become an overriding issue in contemporary America. A thoughtful examination of challenges faced by modern policy makers is illustrative of the ever present conflicts encountered when public interests are posited against private interests.

Public Policy Criteria Examined

1. A public need must be recognized.

It is noteworthy that preservation of the beauty of natural landscapes did not first occur in the eastern United States but rather in the West. Huge open landscapes, giant trees, and enormous mountains would, at first glance, appear to be impossible for humans to reduce in splendor.

Sparsely settled by nomadic *hunter-gatherer* tribes of Native Americans, the magnificent land of the Sierras remained a pristine wilderness unsullied by human settlement. But when gold was discovered in the foothills of the Sierras in 1848, thousands of land-grabbing, immigrant Americans in quest of riches flooded the area. The result was the ruthless theft of land cherished and uncorrupted by Native Americans, who for centuries had left scant evidence of their presence. As miners found gold for the taking in the 1850s, greedy hordes overran the Native Americans, disrupting their lives, slaying and scattering them. This, inevitably, led to armed conflict.[1]

Word of desecration of the land by miners spread to influential Californians who were determined to stop the damage. They petitioned Washington in the 1850s to protect the Sierras, especially Yosemite.[2] It took until 1864, the height of the Civil War, for Washington to respond. Congress deeded Yosemite to California as a state preserve. The Yosemite Grant was signed into law June 30, 1864, by President Abraham Lincoln, giving credence to a new concept: land conservation. Acquiring scenic United States landscapes was deemed in the public interest.

While discouraging development in Yosemite, California nonetheless did license grazing, farming, and logging within the confines of the preserve without incident until John Muir (1838–1914), a visionary Scottish immigrant, visited the land of Yosemite and the Sierras. He was confounded by the California policy permitting livestock grazing, especially grazing by domestic sheep, within the parameters of the preserve. He saw the policy as a grave threat to the natural character of the land. He called the sheep "hoofed locusts" and championed a campaign to institute prudent protection and preservation of the land for all time. Seeking support, he invited a friend, Robert Underwood Johnson, editor of the widely circulated *Century Magazine*, to join him on a camping trip to Yosemite. On the trip, he had little difficulty persuading Johnson of the damage resulting from the flawed policy. Johnson published two passionate articles by Muir in 1890 in which Muir detailed the problem and proffered a solution. The articles, together with other equally passionate appeals for conservation, gained national attention and the unchallenged position for Muir as father of the national parks.

Muir proclaimed there should be no observable intrusion on pristine wilderness. He viewed grazing or gathering timber as a violation of the intent to conserve and protect the land. Muir's efforts were unflagging. In 1892, he organized the first environmental organization, the Sierra Club, to support his efforts. He lobbied President Teddy Roosevelt to keep the wilderness pure, pristine, and without "domesticated animals or Indians," revealing the racial bias of his time. Years later, he came to understand the bland effect of Native Americans on the land when he spent a summer living among them.[3] In

1906, Muir's desire for greater control over land use of Yosemite prevailed. Four decades after Lincoln granted Yosemite to California, Muir persuaded President Teddy Roosevelt to assume federal control of Yosemite.[4] California ceded its authority back to the feds, whereupon Yosemite became a national park, among the first of much federally owned land.

2.   A plan to meet the need must be developed.

Following the lead of the federal government's creation of the national park system, individual states began to recognize the importance of preserving land and establishing parks. Many eighteenth- and nineteenth-century cities and towns throughout the United States centered around public parks or commons, but designating rural areas for parks within states or counties was unheard of at the time. The entry of states into the land preservation arena put the exclusive use policy Muir advocated to the test.

Gifford Pinchot (1865–1946), a member of President Teddy Roosevelt's cabinet and later governor of Pennsylvania, was among Muir's many friends and supporters, but Pinchot locked horns with his longtime friend over Muir's rigid conservation policy. The disagreement caused a permanent estrangement between the two men as well as a new land policy. Pinchot, the charismatic Pennsylvania governor, asserted a more liberal philosophy. In Pinchot's view, conservation should "produce the greatest good, for the greatest number, for the longest run." Pinchot thrived on public debate and argued ardently for responsible logging and grazing policies. He was prescient in his concern about pollution and the need for affordable, sustainable energy sources. In league with Teddy Roosevelt, Pinchot prevailed over Muir and gained support for multiuse national and state parks by including not only conservation, but preservation, environmentalism, and tourism as part of the evolving land policy.

In recognition of his policy achievements for the nation and the Pennsylvania Commonwealth, a 2,338-acre state park surrounding a 340-acre lake in York County bears his name. The Gifford Pinchot State Park is a prime attraction, but the argument that began between Muir and Pinchot continues to this day at the federal, state, and local level. Using public land for oil drilling, logging, and mining is opposed by defenders of preservation who seek to protect land created by the hand of God from the reckless hands of men. Debates over government land acquisition practices persist to the present. How is the imposition of land acquisition, especially eminent domain, balanced with individual property rights? When do public interests override individual interests?

A policy outgrowth of the Pennsylvania State Park System was the State Conservation Commission, established in 1945 to work cooperatively with local, state, and federal government agencies, industry, professional associations, and nonprofit organizations to ensure the wise use of Pennsylvania's natural resources through conservation of soil, water, and related resources.[5] Strip farming practices, widely employed at the time, and the resultant soil erosion, drew attention to the need for soil conservation policies. Farmers throughout the state were encouraged to adopt contour farming methods to conserve valuable topsoil. The commission established and presided over districts throughout the state.

Oversight of parks and forests was the domain of a York County man, Samuel S. Lewis (1874–1959). A single-minded Republican Party boss, Lewis was dedicated to public land preservation. He served as Pennsylvania lieutenant governor in the Arthur H. James administration (1939–1943), then as Secretary of the Department of Forests and Waters (1951–1954), gaining administrative oversight of all state parks and forests. In two years, he reorganized and streamlined the department. His leadership was legendary. Totally committed to land preservation, Lewis donated a thirty-five-acre parcel from his own farm in York County to the Commonwealth in 1954. He persuaded Walter Stine, a neighbor, to sell his arboretum to the Commonwealth. He then exercised his considerable political talent to convince the Commonwealth to buy another farm adjacent to the initial park tract to round out the park. The result of Lewis's gift, situated 885 feet above sea level, is a magnificent eighty-five-acre state park atop Mt. Pisgah, a high point in York County. The Samuel Lewis State Park tenders a spectacular panoramic daytime view of the Susquehanna River meandering across fertile farmlands peppered with quaint towns. At night, the park commands an uninterrupted view of the stars. It can't be denied that there is no more appropriate reminder of a visionary man to be found than this land given to the ages by Sam Lewis.

3. A source of funding must be available.

At the conclusion of World War II, the six-day workweek was reduced to five, establishing a forty-hour workweek, creating time for leisure and money for automobile travel on the expanding road system. One of the results of newfound leisure and roads was increased use of state parks, along with an added demand for more state parks for citizens seeking sanctuaries from urban stress. To address the need in 1955, the inaugural year of Governor George Leader's term, the native son of York County earmarked royalties from oil and gas taken from state-owned land for conservation and land acquisition. He was deeply committed to land conservation and recreation. Seeking professionalism in his administration and the elimination of political appointments, he turned to Maurice K. Goddard, asking him, an ardent conservationist and then head of The Pennsylvania State University Forestry School, to help establish priorities. He subsequently appointed Goddard as Secretary of the Department of Forests and Waters. Goddard's tenure extended over twenty-four years and six governors, affirming the wisdom of Leader's selection. His credentials were stellar: University of Maine, B.S. Forestry; University of California at Berkley, M.S. Forestry; Lt. Colonel U.S. Army (1941–1945), Bronze Star and Legion of Merit; Mt. Alto Forestry School, Director. Among the priorities Goddard established during the Leader administration was a goal of a state park within twenty-five miles of every resident of Pennsylvania. In effect, the potential was a state park system comprised of 175 parks. Acquisition began immediately. Goddard reorganized the Bureau of State Parks into four geographic regions, which remain unchanged at this writing. Park usage under Goddard rose from eight million in 1955 to twenty-four million annual visitors in 1961. He traveled throughout the state advancing the goal of parks within twenty-five miles of every resident.

left to right P. Joseph Raab, Philip Glatfelter, Maurice Goddard, Harry McLaughlin visiting lake site

Maurice Goddard was prophetic when he asserted "Acquiring parks and open spaces for parks in and around urban centers must be regarded as a 'now or never' proposition … such a program simply cannot be postponed until sometime in the remote and hazy future, because land costs in these areas, high as they are now, will be too high for government purchase in another ten years." The acquisition aims of Maurice Goddard were advocated to anyone who would listen.

The legislature supported Goddard's idea with a bond issue, Project 70, to raise money for forestry, conservation, parks, improved water quality, and pollution control. The bond went through the Pennsylvania House of Representatives and the Senate, and was approved by voters in 1963. Goddard never reached his twenty-five-mile goal, but his vision became the cornerstone of county parks in Pennsylvania. A significant result of Project 70 at the state level was the impoundment of the Codorus Creek in York County. Philip Glatfelter, Fortune 500 CEO of the family-owned Glatfelter Paper Company in Spring Grove, proposed a cooperative project with the Commonwealth. Glatfelter planned to furnish the water supply needs of his company while, at the same time, providing water for the town of Spring Grove and a public recreation area adjacent to the impoundment. The first of its kind in the United States, the innovative project was launched by Glatfelter's investment of $5.5 million in the dam. Its gates closed to impound water in 1966. The Commonwealth acquired the park land with Project 70 land acquisition funds during 1965–1966. Park facilities were funded by Project 500 together with a Pennsylvania bond program supplemented with money from the federal government's Land and Water Conservation Fund. Codorus State Park was the first Project 500 program in the state and was the model for public-private partnerships throughout the nation.

Project 70 funds were appealing to county governments and motivated county officials to put apparatuses in place to enhance their eligibility. The first step for eligibility was the creation of planning commissions. In 1965, the third York County Planning Director since the Commission's inception in 1959 was retained by the York County Commissioners. The shy, scholarly director, Jack Dunn, thoughtfully undertook his task and, aided by a small support staff, began studying the demographics of York County. He assessed needs and formulated recommendations, all of which were routinely presented to the County Commissioners, but seldom acted upon.

Planning Director Jack Dunn

One of the conclusions of his research was the need in the county for open public space for the growing population. Dunn, like all planners, was a visionary, but even armed with evidence to support his visions, he faced politicians who were, for the most part, pragmatic. But Dunn's voice was not the only one calling attention to the need and desirability of land acquisition for public open space—parks. City recreation legend Sylvia Newcombe called attention to the critical need for land for parks and recreation to serve the rapidly expanding population growing beyond the boundaries of the city of York. Her cries also fell on deaf ears, but all of that was about to change.

4. A dynamic leader must advocate the benefits.

P. Joseph Raab

Joseph P. Raab was a country kid, a York county kid, a farmer's son who grew up swinging on old tractor tires suspended from trees, toiling in farm fields, hunting rabbits, swimming in creeks, and picnicking in churchyards after Sunday worship. Nothing very noteworthy unless you try and understand how a boy reared in an agricultural wonderland would, as a man, become an advocate of publicly owned parks in the country. The answer, perhaps, lies in his dedication to public service and love of the land, matched with innate leadership skills and an open mind. In 1968, Raab was elected president of the York County Board of Commissioners, a role he thoroughly enjoyed, but it was not the modest salary that motivated Joe to leave his thriving Dallastown orchards for the demands of a county commissioner.[6] It was, undoubtedly, his dedication to public service, matched by his commitment to preserving and protecting the beautiful place he called home.

Stewardship was important to Raab. Now Dunn had an ear. Raab devoured every bit of information Dunn supplied from the Planning

Commission Office. Envisaging the growth projected for the sleepy county's future was hard, but Dunn backed up each projection with carefully gathered demographics for the anticipated rampant growth patterns. The challenge of preserving the quality of life in the county during a time of dynamic growth would require persuading seventy-two disparate townships and boroughs within the county to enact zoning ordinances—a revolutionary idea in rural, agricultural communities unaccustomed to land use planning, let alone regulation. Planning Commission reports indicated *public* stewardship would be essential in communities that were exceedingly proud of their own dutiful, *private* stewardship of the farms that occupied most of the land in the county.

Although York County was a dynamic manufacturing hub, growth had been negligible, and development, until then, was largely clustered around the fringes of York city, Hanover, and the West Shore. The new interstate highway, I-83, crossed the undulating hills from north to south, transporting travelers "through" but seldom "to" destinations in York County. Old Route 30, the Lincoln Highway, continued to serve as the best east-west route between Gettysburg and Lancaster, a trip brief enough to preclude even a coffee stop in York. Dunn's projections of exponential growth as a result of the interstate were hard for Raab to imagine. However, as Dunn continued to describe the importance of acquiring and preserving land for parks, recreation, and conservation, he recognized an ally in Raab, who declared he would dedicate himself to the recommendations of the Planning Commission—and he did.[7]

5.   A positive public response must be elicited.

Raab wasted no time. Encouraged by the availability of state and federal funds and supported by the Planning Commission recommendations and a county task force, A Better Community (ABC), he moved forward at the beginning of 1968 with the full accord of his fellow County Commissioners. The County Commissioners' attention had been drawn to an undeveloped parcel five miles east of York city that was available for sale, a prime location for a park for the rapidly expanding suburban population as well as the underserved citizens of the city of York. Raab, always armed with charm and ample sacks of apples from the fertile fields of his orchards, met with members of the family-owned property and determined it to be a suitable site for a county park—as a matter of fact, an ideal location.

The possibility of a county park set the stage for the next step, formation of the York County Board of Parks and Recreation. In the enthusiastic style for which he was noted, he enlisted community leaders who shared his love of York County, open space, and people. His selection criteria required geographic representation. The board would be composed of people from throughout the 911-square-mile county to guarantee representation of each area. He also selected individuals with a variety of talents and interests: conservation, preservation, recreation, history, and vision. Were he to have received a grade for his personnel skills, it would have to have been an "A." The selection criteria Raab implemented continue to serve the county well and are basically unaltered. His appointees came from all walks of life. Many, like the general population, were native born. They shared values of thrift, were cautious, and were not prone to impulsive decision making; but they were, advisedly, universally committed to acquiring as much land as possible, for as little as possible, as soon as possible, to guarantee unadulterated open space from that time forward. The cautious neophyte board did not take the beauty of the spacious land for granted. They made it their mission to protect significant amounts of county land from unplanned growth and development. They were visionaries, as were those who followed—a surprise even to themselves.

The Founding Board Memberss

Besides family, not much gave **Phil Stinger** more pleasure than casting a line into the cool water of the Codorus Creek and reeling in a feisty trout, unless it was walking in the woods with his favorite dog in pursuit of a cottontail or pheasant. Stinger didn't just take from the land and water as president of the Izaak Walton League; he was a hands-on leader, stocking streams and ponds with trout, bluegills, and sonnies, and lobbying other outdoor enthusiasts to care for the woods. He made a mission of spreading the message of prudence and conservation. Joe Raab recognized him as a prime candidate for the new board and, as in each case of board selection, he was a good choice. Stinger's board tenure was brief, a one-year term, but effective.[8] Ironically, the conclusion of his term coincided with his death. On surrendering his seat at the March 1969 board meeting, he said, "It has been a pleasure to work with the members of this board, whom I consider allies of conservation." His widow accepted a certificate of appreciation for his dedicated service at the April 1969 board meeting.

Harry McLaughlin was a hard-driving newsman with the curiosity of a cat and the memory of an elephant. Editor of the York edition of the *Harrisburg Patriot News,* he lived in the suburbs outside York city. A dedicated family man, who encouraged sportsmanship as well as academic achievement in his children, McLaughlin knew everybody and could engage anybody. His scoops were enviable. He loved politics, people, and public parks. Harry was among Raab's first choices.[9]

Hanover was represented by **Carroll C. Luckenbaugh**, senior pastor of Trinity United Church of Christ and an active member of the Hanover Community Progress Council Recreation Committee. A quiet, reflective man with impressive listening skills, he brought a temperate approach to the energetic board, making him well liked and easy to admire. Luckenbaugh grew up in North Codorus Township near Spring Grove, the second child of a loving, stable family with deep roots in the community. During his childhood, he and his elder sister loved biking the back roads of the county. Recognized early for his leadership ability, Luckenbaugh was elected president of Spring Grove High Student Council and composed the school alma mater. His only years away from York County were in pursuit of his degree at Franklin and Marshall College, followed by Seminary. Following ordination, he returned to serve the Trinity congregation in Hanover at the age of twenty-nine, married a local girl, a York Hospital maternity room nurse, and with her reared three children. Of the many contributions Luckenbaugh brought to the board, none was more unusual than the means he employed to locate a water supply for Rocky Ridge County Park. Efforts to drill a well had proven fruitless until Luckenbaugh invited a friend, Willy Reichart, to locate water. The two men walked the park, and Reichart tapped his divining rod every so often until, at last, he declared, he had found water. A well was drilled on the designated spot, confirming Reichart's ability. Luckenbaugh also took Reichart to Apollo County Park, where he identified and marked a suitable location for a well, which is as yet undrilled. Whether the success of the water quest was Luckenbaugh's divine inspiration or Reichart's divining rod remains undetermined.[10]

Sylvia Newcombe, the farsighted leader of the York City Recreation and Parks Commission, was a natural choice. Highly respected, Newcombe was a seasoned professional who, better than any, understood the importance and the urgency of acquiring land for public recreation and parks. Long an advocate of going beyond the bounds of the city to extend outdoor opportunities to growing numbers of children outside the city limits, she was a valuable addition. Newcombe had labored for parks and recreation her entire professional life. She arrived in York and assumed the role of Director of York City Recreation and Parks in the fall of 1932 as a twenty-seven-year-old filled with zeal. She had completed graduate studies and, ever the student, spent the summer of 1932 at the University of North Carolina studying drama. The York City Recreation and Parks Department was fortunate to have a board filled with industrial leaders. One, Robert Turner, CEO of New York Wire Cloth, expressed his concern that a single woman have proper living arrangements. He asked if her mother would be accompanying her. A very independent woman, Newcombe explained that she had found suitable housing with an elderly lady in York. She dedicated the rest of her life to York, orchestrating playground programs, parks outings, parades, and athletic competitions, and was artful in producing great results with very limited budgets. She advocated preventative direction for young people focusing on guidance in wholesome pursuits. She made her role one of establishing a healthy community through the use of parks and recreation programs to address and prevent social ills that inevitably led to social decline.[11]

Kerr Anderson was a businessman, born in Winterstown, and reared, from his third year, on a family farm in Airville. An only child, Kerr occupied the days of his childhood with his beloved pets. His favorite, a dog, Mete, was a devoted German Shepherd who followed her young master around the farm or followed behind the sleigh that drew Anderson to the one-room school on snowy days. A mature child, Kerr carried water from the well and stoked the coal stove of the spartan classroom, where he eagerly attended to his lessons. When he graduated from Red Lion High School, he continued his education at Lancaster Business School before returning to Sunnyburn and launching a garage and service station business, where he repaired farm equipment and autos for the local farming community. He married his high school sweetheart and, when he wasn't occupied at home or with business, devoted many years of service to the York County Conservation Society, serving for a time as president. In time he assumed management of Yorktowne Mutual Insurance, an agency his father founded. He was also a bank director of the former National Central Bank of Red Lion. A modest man, Anderson, nonetheless, reserved bragging rights for his two children, which was apparent when he spoke of his son, an engineer who played a prominent role in the moon launch, or his daughter, a design and production manager for the University Press at the University of Virginia. His parks involvement began on a cold day in early 1968 when he headed to the courthouse on business. As he ascended the marble stairs, he was waylaid by Joe Raab. Raab explained that Anderson's business acumen was essential for the new Parks Board. As usual, leaving no opportunity for reflection, Raab essentially drafted Anderson for board service on the spot. Uncertain of the commitment at first, it did not take Kerr Anderson long to become one of the most dedicated members and an ardent proponent of the immense satisfaction to be derived from board service.[12]

Ray Wiegand was a small man with a big heart, a professional Boy Scout executive, with an abiding love of kids and camping. Like Newcombe, Wiegand brought a wide range of experience to his role on the board and required no persuasion to join its ranks. An essential part of his Boy Scout experience would serve him well: knowing how to do a lot with a little and how to promote projects by extending hospitality. Wiegand and his wife lived just outside the city and recognized the importance of wholesome recreation opportunities for the growing population of York County.[13]

Voni Grimes was born black in Bamburg, South Carolina, an unenviable station for a boy in times of segregation and bigotry. When Grimes was two years old, his father followed a brother-in-law to York for work and better opportunities for his family. It is an open question as to how much better the opportunities in York may have been at the time: his elementary school, Smallwood, was segregated; the neighborhood around Susquehanna Avenue, where his family lived, was segregated; and most available jobs for blacks were menial. But Grimes was never defined by his circumstances. He was reared in faith and gifted with a gentle nature and an undiminished determination to do his best for himself and others. He deeply respected the example of his parents and others who labored tirelessly despite barriers. Like Newcombe, Grimes was acutely aware of the fundamental needs of children, especially minorities. When he graduated from William Penn in 1942, he was well-prepared for college but could not afford the $250 annual tuition to attend the school of his choice, Wilberforce. Instead, he left for a paid sheet metal apprenticeship in Philadelphia. When his training was complete, he was inducted into the all-black 92nd Infantry Division of the U.S. Army. He served in the Pacific theater. At the end of the war, he came home to York with established goals: to own his own house by age twenty-five, to move into his dream house by age fifty, to live in the segregated Yorktowne Hotel by age seventy-five, and to be involved in his community. He attained each goal. He became a foreman at Cole Steel and gave generously of his time to the York community, devoting years to enlisting support for recreational activities for city youth. He and Sylvia Newcombe worked together and became a formidable team. As the board was being assembled, Raab approached Grimes and asked him to give of himself again, this time as a member of the new Parks Board. Grimes never needed coaxing and gladly put his energy and considerable human relations skills to work again on behalf of the community.[14]

Carroll Hunt hailed from the south central part of the county. He was born on a farm in New Freedom. His mother died when he was six months old, leaving his father to care for him by himself for several years. When Hunt's father remarried, Hunt became the eldest of five siblings, who began arriving with regularity. As he grew, he helped his parents with the younger children and worked on the farm until he left to obtain a teaching certificate from Millersville State Teachers College. He married his childhood sweetheart, and when her parents were ready to retire, Carroll and Irene bought their farm in Rinely. The Hunts worked the farm, and Carroll taught school throughout the county. He coached basketball, and he taught math at Dallastown High and

Kennard-Dale High. He was an active member of the York County Farmers Association, which is where Raab saw his ability. At a Farmers Association meeting, Raab approached Hunt about the new board. Known as a quiet man of few words, Hunt told Raab he'd give it some thought and get back to him. Twenty minutes later, Raab was back, asking what he had decided. Hunt, like most others, succumbed to Raab's enthusiasm. Hunt loved the verdant land of his native York County and recognized the intrinsic value of preserving open space years before it was a popular idea. Hunt also felt he could dispel a commonly held notion that farmers were disinterested in land beyond the boundaries of their farms by serving on the new board.[15]

Raab, a skillful politician, wanted a representative voice for labor and turned to **Jack Barnhart,** a local labor leader, who had the added advantage of being a resident of York city. A practical, no-nonsense man, Barnhart was known to seek level playing fields for people, whether in life or in a park.[16]

From the northern corner of the county, **John Rinehart** was enlisted. An industrial engineer at the Steelton office of the Bethlehem Steel plant, Rinehart, as many other residents of the West Shore, lived in what was a commuter community, a bedroom community for those who worked outside the county. He was concerned about the rapid expansion of residential development along Pennsylvania Route 15 and understood the importance of wholesome recreational resources for young and old citizens.[17]

6.   An administrative or legislative mandate must vest authority for policy implementation into accountable, competent, dedicated hands in a timely way.

In no time, Joe Raab had assembled the members of the new board. It was composed of representatives from all walks of life: public, private, not for profit, business, agriculture, management, and labor. It had, as well, delegates from all the geographic areas of the large county. The assignment was clear: acquire land for conservation and recreation without delay. The players were cast; the stage was set.

Chapter 2
1968–1977: Acquisition

o o o o o o o o o o o o o o o o o o o o o o o o o o o o o o o o o o o

Everybody needs beauty as well as bread, places to play in and pray in where nature may heal and cheer and give strength to the body and soul.

John Muir
(1838–1914)

The Beginning

On April 18, 1968, no man had, as yet, set foot on the moon, and unreported challenges facing the upcoming Apollo moon mission were making the prospect of the mission questionable.[18] Martin Luther King had been dead for two weeks and racial tensions fomenting throughout the nation had exploded in violent conflicts. President Lyndon B. Johnson announced, only a few weeks before, that he would not seek reelection; the war in Vietnam raged, and anti-war sentiment divided the country.

But turbulent times seemed far away on what was a glorious clear spring evening in York. The seventy-seven-degree daytime temperature swiftly dropped into the fifties as the sun set.[19] Hyacinths overflowed the planters along Market Street, permeating the night air with their distinctive fragrance. Daffodils in stone urns punctuated landings on the austere marble courthouse stairs, seemingly dancing in rhythm to a gentle breeze. At 7:45 p.m. in a second-floor meeting room, Joe Raab jubilantly tapped the gavel summoning the inaugural meeting of the York County Board of Parks and Recreation to order as the twenty-ninth county parks and recreation commission in Pennsylvania.

Transforming Ideas into Action

The agenda for the first meeting was not complicated. The new board had no budget, no structure, no staff, no office, no parks, and few citizens who gave much thought to planting parks where potatoes grew. But the board did have responsibility. In confirmation of the obligations being assumed by the newly assembled members, Joe Raab read the resolution of the York County Commissioners establishing the York County Board of Parks and Recreation as an advisory arm. He followed the resolution by reading Article XXV, Section 2501, of the Pennsylvania County Code, the enabling legislation granting counties authority to acquire land and real estate by "gift, purchase, the power of eminent domain, or by lease within the boundaries within the county."

The administrative bones of the board took shape that evening with the election of officers:

> President: Harry McLaughlin
> Vice President: Carroll Luckenbaugh
> Secretary: Sylvia Newcombe
> Treasurer: Voni Grimes

Though no funds were budgeted by the county, money was available. Native son Henry Leader, staff advisor to his brother, Governor George Leader, led the struggle for enactment of Pennsylvania Act 256 in 1955. The legislation earmarked oil and gas royalties from state-owned land for conservation, recreation, and land acquisition. Among the first state parks to benefit from the fund was land in northern York County, the Gifford Pinchot State Park.[20] The oil and gas revenue stream was innovative and precedent setting, but insufficient to meet the ambitious goals of Secretary of Forests and Waters Maurice Goddard. In order to facilitate his aims, he advanced two ambitious state bond issues for forestry, conservation, parks, water conservation, and pollution abatement in the early 1960s. The first project was approved during the Lawrence administration in 1961, setting the ambitious plan in motion. A state constitutional amendment was required to authorize an increase to the state debt limit, which was, at the time, capped at $1 million. Goddard's other proposal was for a $70 million bond initiative to be expended by 1970, dubbing the second project with the inevitable title "Project 70." Governor Lawrence appealed to the legislature to put the referendum on the ballot. In spite of the enormity of the request and considerable opposition, the legislature approved the request, while adding another ballot question calling for a constitutional convention.

Each proposal was a bold political move. Constitutional amendments require voter approval in two consecutive separately elected sessions of the legislature. The first approval of Project 70 as a ballot issue occurred during the Democratic Lawrence administration; the second, a year later, during the first term of Governor Scranton, a Republican. Demonstrable evidence of Secretary Goddard's influence was his retention by Governor Scranton despite the open criticism Goddard leveled at many of Scranton's policies. Recognizing Goddard's political acumen and the timeliness of the proposal, Governor Scranton not only retained Goddard, he embraced Project 70. Under Scranton's leadership, Project 70 passed the Senate unanimously and the House by a vote of 174 to 14. On election day, November 5, 1963, when Project 70 came before the electorate, over two million voters entered the polls to cast ballots. The question for a Pennsylvania Constitutional Convention passed. Project 70 also passed, but by a very slim 113,000-vote margin. Governor Scranton signed Act 8 into law June 22, 1964, establishing the legal blueprint for Project 70 expenditures. The accompanying bill streamlined eminent domain property proceedings and set the wheels in motion. Three state parks were immediately approved: Ohiopyle (Fayette and Somerset Counties); Tyler (Bucks County); and Codorus (York County).

Funding at the federal level became available at about the same time. It grew out of the Eisenhower administration's goal of establishing parks for recreational day trips within an hour of every urban center in the United States. The policy resulted in the Land and Water Conservation Fund, which was enacted into law during the Johnson administration. This program was funded by income from offshore oil and gas drilling in the Gulf of Mexico. Ultimately, $300–$900 million was expended from the offshore income, most during the mid-1960s. Pennsylvania received $100 million.

Half of the Pennsylvania share of the fund was administered by the Department of Community Affairs for the development of urban, township, and county parks. The other half was administered by the Department of Forests and Waters. Secretary Goddard put a formula in place allocating four-sevenths of the fund to state parks, one-seventh to the Game Commission, one-seventh to the Fish Commission, and one-seventh to the Historical and Museum Commission. The intricate division of funds made grant applications a jigsaw puzzle.

Goddard had advocated public land acquisition for years, declaring delay would eventually make land acquisition cost prohibitive. As public funds became available, it was propitious for counties to take advantage of the new funding streams that mandated an essential criterion, the establishment of a County Board of Parks and Recreation. The availability of the money was not lost on the York Commissioners, especially Joe Raab, who, with the state and federal money in mind, was already seeking suitable land for acquisition.

Raab informed the new board of the parkland acquisition negotiations already in progress. The first, a privately-owned property five miles east of the city of York, would, in time, become Rocky Ridge County Park. Another larger parcel, located in the southeastern quadrant of the county, was an agricultural area that would, in the future, become Spring Valley County Park.

Energized by Raab's enthusiasm, the new board gave its support by endorsing the effort to acquire the parcel east of the city of York. The outcome of the acquisition would be contingent upon the availability of federal and state funding. The county would not act without the support of the state and federal money.[21] The board also opted to initiate efforts to acquire the second parcel before federal and state funds became unavailable.

With acquisition of one site in progress and another under consideration, Raab emphasized the urgency of submitting proposals for state and federal appropriations before the funding well ran dry. The importance of convening meetings quickly to preclude missed opportunities caused newly elected chairman McLaughlin to sagely suggest structuring the board with task forces. The benefits of the task force model were apparent: ease and speed of assembly matched by a specific purpose. A single focus equips a task force to gather information and make recommendations quickly. The task force model is more formal than an *ad hoc* committee, and lacks the disadvantages of committees, which are prone to digress, delay, debate, and easily become mired in detail. The task force approach was exactly right. The outcome was, and continues to be, a vibrant board.

With board support, Joe Raab continued to serve as point man in negotiations. He charmed sellers, dispelled the concerns of neighbors, addressed legal concerns, and made frequent progress reports to the Board of Commissioners and the Parks Board. Public land acquisition is complicated, and acquisition of Rocky Ridge County Park was sufficiently complex that the Parks Board opted to table requests for funding for the second parcel in the southeastern part of the county until they were further along with the first. That acquisition was also thwarted, at the time, because one of the criteria for funds was unmet.

Eligibility for funding was predicated on planning commissions. North Hopewell Township, one of the venues under consideration, did not have a township planning commission. North Hopewell supervisors readily agreed to create a planning commission, which set the wheels in motion for acquisition of the second parcel, which would become Spring Valley County Park. At the time, the area was identified as Rehmeyer's Hollow, a misnomer since the land under consideration was actually located in Blymire's Hollow.

**Martin Kondor at future site of first county park,
Rocky Ridge County Park**

The first parcel, east of the city, first known as the Kondor tract, was an unspoiled family-owned woodland ridge slated to become the first county park. But there would be countless hoops through which to leap before that day. Weaving through federal and state guidelines for land acquisition was an ongoing challenge for the neophyte board. Title searches, aerial surveys, planners, soil conservation authorities, consultants, architects, citizens, and local, county, state, and federal officials were involved each step of the way. Each agency brought its own, frequently divergent, views to the table. Addressing the requirements and considerations of each funding source created an environment of confusion that would deter any but the most dedicated grant seeker. Among the unanticipated concerns associated with the acquisition of Rocky Ridge County Park were an unsanitary landfill adjacent to the site, survey lines that did not meet, and groups lobbying for special park usage—hunting, motorcycles, snowmobile trails, horseback riding, ski areas, and camping, to name a few. Practical concerns revolved around entrances, roads, signs, traffic flow, parking, and the myriad other details associated with the planning and design of a public facility.

What would be best for the *public interest,* not *special interest,* was foremost in the minds of the cautious board. Any special use of parkland was subject to stringent criteria, which were based on balancing the impact of the use on the overall effect on the land. A clear example of the board approach was hiking trails. Obviously trails are desirable in parks, but they would be designed to do no harm: erosion, stream damage, and encroachment on unique geology sites would be among the primary considerations of trail design. This board policy has been effectively employed and affords a broad range of park use without adverse consequences to the land—the mark of prudent management policies.

Here They Come

In no time, word of the new Parks and Recreation Board was out, not in small measure because of enthusiastic promotion by members, especially Harry McLaughlin. Ever the cheerleader for York County, McLaughlin heralded the new parks and recreation effort in print and in person. His promotion of parks garnered the attention of legendary Olympic weight-lifting icon and marketing genius, Bob Hoffman, a native son and CEO of York Barbell.

York Barbell founder Bob Hoffman

From its inception, offers of land found their way to the Parks Board. Each was thoughtfully considered. The board drew on recommendations of the York County Planning Commission, as well as its own careful judgment, to weigh each opportunity. Throughout its acquisition phase, the board identified management responsibilities. A paramount goal of the board was to establish parks throughout the county, but no less important were considerations for the security of land, water, people, and wildlife in any park site. Stewardship ranked high on the priority list of the board.

Evidence of the need for park security was apparent. As parkland came into the system, it created an added burden for townships to provide regular police services on the new public land. As ongoing incidents of vandalism occurred, it was obvious that leaning on local municipalities for enforcement of rules and regulations was faulty. But by law, the Parks Department lacked authority to enforce rules and regulations governing the parks. State Representative Raymond Hovis introduced legislation to alleviate the problem by sponsoring House Bill 2088 in 1972. The aim of the bill was to amend the county code to grant third- to eighth-class counties the power to impose fines and jail sentences. York, a third-class county, would benefit by passage. Enactment of the new law allowed parks departments to enforce park rules and regulations and to make arrests for violations, which would be heard by district magistrates for disposition. Penalties up to one-hundred-dollar fines and/or ten-day jail sentences could be imposed. Following enactment of Bill 2088, the York County Parks Director and Superintendent were deputized as sheriffs.

Having a better handle on park security, the board continued its quest for land. Bob Hoffman's offer consisted of a potential gift of 176 acres just outside the town of Jacobus. The Hoffman tract contained one caveat, however, which was dependent on the board granting Hoffman permission to name the park. This was not an overriding issue, so pursuit of the gift was undertaken with dispatch. Consultations with soil and water conservation experts, local officials, the highway department, historians, naturalists, educators, county officials, and the Audubon Society resulted in approval of the offer. In the end, there was, no doubt, surprise when Hoffman informed the board of the name he had chosen for the Park. It was commonly thought he would dub it the "Bob Hoffman Park," but to the chagrin of some and the surprise of many, he named it in honor of the newly-elected president of the United States, Richard M. Nixon. It is perhaps the first and only park to bear the name of the former president.

President Nixon's elderly Quaker parents had led quiet, low-profile lives in their home outside the nearby hamlet of East Berlin and would, no doubt, have been very pleased with the name designation. Harry McLaughlin used his feature column to extol Hoffman, the County Parks, and the Nixon connection. When the president ultimately visited the park in 1988, he graciously heaped praise on what had been done in his name. By the time of his visit, the Richard M. Nixon County Park had become an environmental education center. Supported by assistance from the Audubon Society, the center is a unique county contribution to environmental education for young and old and a model facility. Nixon's visit generated extensive press coverage for his namesake, the small jewel of a park.

left to right President Richard Nixon, P.Joseph Raab, Voni Grimes

Another park prospect, the Lebovitz tract, emerged from recommendations of a 1960s Community Services survey. The implementation committee of the survey was chaired by a prominent attorney and savvy community activist, Donn I. Cohen. Cohen appealed to the board to consider property bordering the Codorus Creek between West Princess Street and West College Avenue in York city. The Lebovitz tract was fraught with complications. A 1958 study, the "Rotival Report," prepared by renowned French urban planner Maurice Rotival, detailed improvements along the Codorus Creek to spur renewal in a rapidly deteriorating area of York city. The Rotival Report was ahead of its time.[22]

One recommendation involved the creation of a pedestrian mall on West Market Street between Pershing Avenue and George Street to stimulate business in the downtown shopping district. The downtown was experiencing a tumultuous decline as one after another commercial enterprise left the city due to insufficient parking. The Rotival plan eliminated automobile traffic on Market Street between George and Pershing to create a pedestrian mall. Large, convenient parking areas were to be established behind the Market Street shops and businesses along the alleyways to the rear. At the time, the report was thought laughable by city fathers and the public. In retrospect, it was brilliant by any measure, but by the time the full measure of the parking dilemma was understood, the York Mall, located east of the city, had sapped the downtown business away, never to return, leading to further deterioration of the city and other areas such as the Lebovitz tract.

Racial tensions in the city were escalating by 1968. In an attempt to stem incidents, an afterschool program known as the 3:10 Club was in place on the Lebovitz tract. A Community Services survey affirmed the prudence of stemming the rising tide of resentment springing from lack of well-developed community resources. Persuading public officials to invest in a perilous area of the city was, however, fraught with political ramifications that undoubtedly kept the Parks Board from taking on the thorny issues associated with the project. Today a park is located on the site under the aegis of the York City Recreation Department.

Donn I. Cohen and industrialist-philanthropist Louis Appell urged the board to merge the existing recreational authorities of townships and boroughs into subdivisions of the York County Parks Department to add viability to grant requests in accordance with recommendations of the Community Services survey. There was no opposition to the petition, but at the time, there were insufficient means to attempt mergers of separate parks and recreation authorities in addition to meeting the acquisition responsibilities faced by the small, understaffed board. The consolidation of parks and recreation services and facilities is still worthy of consideration and may be undertaken by a future board.

Another proposal hinged around the old York Collegiate Institute gymnasium, forerunner of York Junior College, located on the corner of College Avenue and Duke Street in York city. The Junior College had gained four-year status and bought the grounds of the Outdoor Country Club on Country Club Road in Spring Garden Township. The old gym stood empty and was deteriorating, as was the neighborhood, so a county-run recreation facility was a valid idea to rejuvenate the area.

Undoubtedly, civil unrest in the city of York during the late 1960s and the violent riots of 1969 kept the cautious board from tackling the old York Collegiate Institute (YCI) gym. But board member Voni Grimes, acting independently, was undeterred in his aspirations for the children of York city, and his ongoing, often lonely, efforts ultimately resulted in acquisition of the old gym by the York City Recreation Department. Today the gym has been refurbished and provides an outstanding, large venue for as many as one thousand young and old sports fans at a time. His tireless work in rescuing this unique facility was acknowledged when the old building was rededicated in 1984 as the Voni Grimes Recreation Gymnasium.

A one-dollar ten-year lease on an eighty-five-acre tract outside Stewartstown on Deer Creek was proffered to the Parks Board by local attorney Ross McGinnis. A nine hundred-acre parcel near Fawn Grove and Peach Bottom Township was also offered for a long-term lease of $500 per acre by yet another lawyer, Judson Ruch.

During this period, innovations in parks and recreation were surfacing throughout the nation. One interesting concept was the conversion of abandoned power lines and railroad beds into linear parks for pedestrians, bicyclists, and equestrians. In 1973, such a proposal came before the board. John Davenport, vice president of the York County Environmental Council, apprised the Parks Board of an Environmental Council study recommending conversion of six miles of the abandoned Pennsylvania Railroad line east of York to Wrightsville Borough into a bike trail. Even though the railroad was in the midst of bankruptcy hearings at the time, which complicated matters, legislation for acquisition of foot and bike trails was underway in the Pennsylvania House, giving the proposal viability. The board was receptive to a linear park from the time of its proposal. Appropriations HB 2528 and SB 116 were slated for the House and Senate in the coming legislative session, earmarking funds from the Motor License Fund for the establishment of foot and bike trails. Ray Wiegand viewed the benefits of the trail for the public as well as his beloved Boy Scouts and moved to support the proposal. Kerr Anderson endorsed Wiegand's motion, which received unanimous consent.

A twenty-five-year lease on six hundred acres along the Susquehanna River on utility-owned land was offered. First leased in 1968 and then donated in 2007, Apollo County Park came into the system by the kindness of the P. H. Glatfelter Pulpwood Company. Named to commemorate the launch of the Apollo Moon mission, it was hoped the significance of the name would attract astronauts or high-ranking politicians to the park dedication. It did neither.

Two small tracts, one twelve-acre and one sixteen-acre parcel, in Carroll Township were offered by Henry Logan and Mary Logan. In addition to the two small parcels, a 120-acre parcel with a stipulated life estate for the Logans was submitted for consideration.

In 1976, Paul Ramsey appeared before the board to appeal for preservation of the home of American poet Lee Anderson (1896–1972).[23] Anderson's house was within the bounds of Spring Valley County Park overlooking a picturesque stocked pond and several outbuildings. In accordance with the request, Grant Voaden and the author submitted the Anderson property to the Pennsylvania Historical and Museum Commission for registration.

Voaden, an engineer and an authority on mills, surveyed and documented every York County mill and millsite. The York County Heritage Trust Museum is the repository of his research. Realizing that Spring Valley County Park had seven millsites within its boundaries, Voaden advocated that the master plan for the park include a working mill. With that in mind, Voaden and the author visited the working mill of Harry Cross, a direct descendant of Alexander Wallace, the earliest miller. The East Hopewell Township mill had been in continuous operation by the same family since the early eighteenth century. The pair proposed to Cross that he give his mill to the county for relocation in Spring Valley County Park. Cross visited the Park and toured the seven sites and was amenable to the suggestion. Voaden and Shoemaker submitted Cross Mill for inclusion in the Pennsylvania Historic Registry. The Wallace-Cross Mill would become part of the Parks System, but not in Spring Valley County Park.

John and Mary Rudy

In 1973, George B. Rudy and Viola Rudy Williams, heirs of the historic Bixler Farmstead, a 143-acre estate situated along the millrace for Mundis Mill, offered the entire parcel, including the 1798 house, summer kitchen, and 1805 barn to the board in memory of their grandparents, John and Mary Rudy, the most recent inhabitants of the rare unspoiled family farm northeast of York city. It would become John Rudy County Park.

Another extraordinary opportunity presented itself to the board when William Kain, then president of the privately owned The York Water Company, offered to share a sixteen hundred-acre parcel of land just south of York city with York County Parks.

Park Construction

The York Water Company was installing two reservoirs (Lake Redman and Lake Williams) on the land in anticipation of York's future water needs. The unique partnership between the county and the privately owned water company was not unlike Codorus State Park in the southwestern part of the county. The only distinction was that the venture would involve a public-private partnership with a county government rather than a state government.

In 1977, a Pennsylvania Department of Transportation study recommended the county of York seek a million-dollar grant in federal funds for a sixty-foot right-of-way over eighteen miles of railroad track for a linear park for bikes, pedestrians, and equestrians. One arm of the proposed route lay between York and Hanover, the other between York and New Freedom, each on the old double-bed railroad, which had been out of service since the floodwaters of Hurricane Agnes destroyed the bridges and many of the rails in 1972.

The plethora of proposals each received careful board review. Recognizing that the appearance of ingratitude or indifference to any land offer could damage the goodwill essential for the board to operate effectively, all board action was taken with discretion, matched with a canny awareness of the importance of choosing only land deemed to be in the best public interest.

Over the course of the first ten years of its existence, the York County Board of Parks and Recreation reviewed every park that would constitute the system except three. Not until 1993 was land offered to the system for what would become the P. Joseph Raab County Park. In 2007, land overlooking the Susquehanna River, concurrent with a federal and state initiative for economic development[24] via cultural tourism, became a park known as Highpoint. It was placed in the hands of the Parks Department without Parks Board review. This was also true of Native Lands County Park, which was part of the much disputed parcel along the Susquehanna River.

In 1968, when Rocky Ridge County Park was acquired, a number of planning steps were put in place that were closely scrutinized by public funding agencies, local officials, the public, parks department staff, and the board. Ray Wiegand, Voni Grimes, Sylvia Newcombe, and Jack Barnhart comprised the Rocky Ridge Task Force. Monies for land acquisition for Rocky Ridge came from the 1965 HUD fund, the Land and Water Conservation Act monies administered by the Pennsylvania Department of Community Affairs, Project 500, and the Pennsylvania Bond, all matched by 25 percent from local taxes, gifts, and bequests. The price to acquire the 760-acre Rocky Ridge County Park in 1968 was $153,000.

During the first ten years of the parks system, Richard M. Nixon County Park was established and developed.

Much of Spring Valley County Park was acquired with grant money and by eminent domain in 1972. The process was implemented by "Declarations of Taking" for all the land and property within the bounds of the park. The process provided a Board of Viewers to determine the values, which were subject to appeal in the Court of Common Pleas. Fifteen houses were condemned in the process. Sadly, although the Lee Anderson House was part of the eminent domain process, it was eventually demolished. The poet's belongings were removed and stored at John Rudy County Park and then turned over to the York County Heritage Trust for safekeeping. The Harry Cross Mill, on the radar from the beginning, was not moved to Spring Valley County Park, but rather became the smallest park site within York County Parks and remained at its original location.

The William H. Kain County Park was established by a fifty-year lease agreement with the York Water Company and entered the parks system in 1976.

William H. Kain

The Heritage Rail Trail became a county park in 1990, when it was purchased from the Commonwealth of Pennsylvania for one dollar. The very first linear park, between York and Hellam, proposed by the environmental study did not come to fruition, but the south and western routes of the old double-bed Penn Central Railroad did, in time, enter the York County Parks as the Heritage Rail Trail County Park.

Every park in the system was selected and most parkland was acquired within the first ten years of the parks' history. The acquisitions as allowed by law were:

by gift:
John Rudy County Park
Richard M. Nixon County Park
Wallace-Cross Mill Historic Site
P. Joseph Raab County Park

by purchase:
Rocky Ridge County Park

by eminent domain and purchase:

Spring Valley County Park

by gift and purchase:
Heritage Rail Trail County Park (for one dollar)

by gift and lease:
William H. Kain County Park

by gift, purchase, and lease:
Apollo County Park

by acquisition and assignment beyond the purview of the York County Department of Parks and Recreation or its board:
Highpoint Scenic Vista and Recreation Area
Native Lands County Park

By 1978, the 904-square-mile County of York had acquired or planned for four thousand acres of parkland. East, west, north, and south York County had three outstanding state parks: Codorus, Pinchot, and Sam Lewis. Eight of the ten York County Parks and the first of ten historic sites (the Bixler Farmstead at John Rudy County Park) and numerous small municipal parks traversed the county. The board had a policy manual in place with well-established guidelines for handling land offers and acquisition.

Budget

The board requested $56,000 for its initial 1969 budget and received $46,000. The very first purchase, $36.60, was a secondhand filing cabinet. It took three years of appeals before Parks Superintendent Duane Close was able to convince the County Commissioners that purchasing a wood chipper rather than leasing one would be cost effective. In 1975, $6,050 was expended for the purchase of the chipper, a basic necessity for any woodland park. A tractor was borrowed from the county of York until the demand exceeded the availability. "Make do" may well have been declared the motto for the financially constrained department.

Revenue

The first revenue resource policy was implemented in 1976. Small fees were charged for the use of picnic shelters at Rocky Ridge County Park.

Structure

The board was in place and functioning with the assistance of task forces and citizen committees, all eager to support York County Parks.

Staff

William Ehrman first Parks Director

Four parks directors served over the course of the first ten years. William Ehrman began his affiliation with the department as an intern in 1968, receiving $750 compensation for six months' work. He also received an auto allowance for travel to various park sites and help from the hourly labor pool of the Community Progress Council and State Employment Office. Ehrman assumed the director's position in 1970, becoming the state's tenth full-time county parks director. He had a full-time secretary and a typewriter.

DUANE CLOSE

Duane Close was retained in 1970 as Parks Superintendent and became director in 1976. Close designed the Nixon County Park Nature Center building, the first parks brochure, and a handsome emblem for the parks.

Parks logo

In 1977, Thomas Krebs occupied the director post until 1978, when Paul Wojciechowski was named to the position. In June 1976, Darryl Albright began a career in law enforcement as a park ranger. His experiences in the parks and later on in municipal police departments led to his election in 2008 as president of the York County Chiefs of Police Association. Albright replaced Philip Trump, who briefly held the position as park ranger. Both Darryl Albright and Thomas Krebs, the first naturalist, were funded through the Comprehensive Employment Training Act (CETA), a federal program.

Office

Board meetings were held in a meeting room at the courthouse until 1973, when they were relocated to John Rudy County Park headquarters. Beginning in November 1968, York County Parks rented office space at the old Duke Street School, 220 South Duke Street, in York with the York County Planning staff for $200 per month. The two departments shared a part-time secretary until the parks office was moved to its permanent administrative offices at John Rudy Park.

The population shift leading to a more suburban landscape had begun, but much of the land in the county was still under cultivation. A vast agricultural county now also contained thousands of acres of parkland. Planting parks where potatoes grew was unusual in the eastern United States. But the farsighted board, led by Joe Raab, continued to look ahead for what was to come, and there would be no regrets.

Chapter 3
1978–1987: Development

o o o o o o o o o o o o o o o o o o o o o o o o o o o o o o o o o o o o o o

It must be believed, because it is true, that people are affected by their environment by space and scale, by color and texture, by nature and beauty, that they can be uplifted, made comfortable, made important.

James W. Rouse
(1914–1996)

There are undeniable, though often unintended, consequences of change. For example, as federal policies change, state and local governments experience the effects of the change, often without the benefit of time to reposition decisions based on the old policies.

The United States Department of the Interior's liberal dispersal of federal and state administered funds for public land acquisition initiated during the Eisenhower administration and carried on throughout the Johnson years began to change during the Nixon administration. The Arab oil embargo in the 1970s resulted in gasoline shortages throughout the United States. The embargo was followed by an economic downturn and a cold, snowy winter, which contributed to the alteration of federal spending policies on parks and parkland. A new philosophy of land use was put into effect.[25] In the late 1970s, federal spending began to center on revenue resourceful projects that included, among other things, support for oil drilling on public land, a complete reversal of the previous policy.

Stewart Udall, U.S. Secretary of the Interior (1961–1969) throughout the Kennedy and Johnson administrations, subscribed to administration goals of acquiring and preserving parkland. Udall deplored attitudes that disregarded the fragile balance of nature, an ecological view based on a modern myth, the ill-conceived notion of "superabundance."[26] Udall was largely responsible for the enactment of environmental laws in Johnson's Great Society legislative agenda, including the Clean Air, Water Quality, and Clean Water Restoration Acts, the Wilderness Act of 1964, the Endangered Species Preservation Act of 1966, the Land and Water Conservation (fund) Act of 1965, the Solid Waste Disposal Act of 1965, the National Trail System Act of 1968, and the Wild and Scenic Rivers Act of 1968. Each of these mandates was designed directly or indirectly to help state and local governments add to and improve public lands and water.

Udall also established policy categories for the acquisition of federal parks based on recommendations emerging from carefully selected Interior Department review panels. He instituted oversight principles and divided land management responsibilities into three areas:

1. **Natural lands such as wilderness** were to be managed to perpetuate and restore the land.
2. **Historic lands such as battlefields or historic homes such as Mount Vernon** were to be managed in just the opposite way, attending first to restoration and then perpetuation.
3. **Recreational land management** was to subordinate natural and historic land considerations to those of public use in order to foster active participation in outdoor recreation in a pleasing environment. Unlike the Udall policy initiative, when James Watt assumed the Interior Department leadership, the federal policies he implemented placed an emphasis on parks paying for themselves.[27]

The Udall management policy included review criteria, which were a valuable aid in acquisition and management of public lands. Interior Department review panels were assembled and remained in effect until 1977, when U.S. Secretary of the Interior Cecil Andrus, a Carter administration appointee, abolished them. Andrus directed the attention of the Park Service to new concepts focusing on parks as tools, economic engines for development, especially in urban settings.

The review panels for land acquisition under Udall included historians, scientists, scholars, and environmentalists. Congress regarded the review panel evaluations very seriously during Udall's tenure. When Andrus eliminated the review panels, the urge for Congress to dip into the undirected largesse of public funds was irresistible. During the Reagan administration (1981–1989), not only were the review panels eliminated but the administration firmly opposed acquisition of any new park sites at all. Republican U.S. 19th

District Congressman George Goodling staunchly bucked the party traces of the Reagan administration and adamantly opposed the new policies.[28] But to no avail. There was no reversal of Reagan's Interior Secretary James Watt's policies.

Lacking Park Service checks and balances by Interior Department review panels, savvy members of Congress recognized a golden opportunity for "Park Barrel" projects. Among them, one egregious example is Steamtown USA in Scranton, Pennsylvania. Regarded by John White, Smithsonian Institute curator of Transportation at the time, as "… a third rate collection located in a place to which it had no relevance … establishing a big railroad museum run by the National Park Service would have been fine, provided some effort had been made to evaluate all the possible sites." None was, yet Congress kept dumping more and more money into it. Then-president of the private National Parks and Conservation Association noted Steamtown as emblematic of a lack of review and planning and emphatically objected to what was happening, saying "The Park Service is a dumping ground, a place where Congress puts things that are not wanted and not needed."

The prudent oversight of the Udall management philosophy, which organized the management of parks, was abandoned in keeping with Secretary James Watt's notion that parks should pay their own way.[29]

York County Parks implemented a management system much like the Udall plan. The plan continues to serve as a responsible approach to park acquisition and management.

The York County parks fall largely within the three management areas outlined by the Udall approach[30]:

1. Apollo County Park and the P. Joseph Raab County Park easily fit the category of Natural Lands.
2. The Wallace-Cross Mill and the Heritage Rail Trail County Park historic sites exist as fine examples of historic land management. At the time the York County system was established, funds for historic sites were acquired with urban renewal money.
3. Rocky Ridge County Park, Richard M. Nixon County Park, John C. Rudy County Park, Spring Valley County Park, William H. Kain County Park, and the Heritage Rail Trail County Park are examples of recreational land management.

In keeping with the federal goals of enhancing coffers with tourist dollars, the Commonwealth designated areas throughout the state as Heritage Regions. The basis of the idea stems from Andrus and later U.S. Secretary of the Interior James Watt, each determined to spur visits to cultural sites to stimulate the economic rewards of tourism dollars. A nature center can convey a natural heritage but, more than a heritage site, the environmental education center at Nixon Park is a superb way to heighten environmental awareness. Perhaps in the future, the reality of Nixon County Park's forward-looking "green" nature will be acknowledged for what it really is: an outstanding example of an educational program dedicated to advancing public knowledge of the fragile nature of the planet—land, sea, air, and all that dwell upon it.

As the challenge of the first decade of the parks was finding and securing land for the new parks department, the second decade was notable for planning and implementing parks with a paucity of money and a plethora of expectations. The effect of state and federal spending policy funding reductions reached state and local park systems at an alarming rate by the late 1970s. Pennsylvania state parks were feeling the pinch and adopted a new approach to shrinking budgets by raising fees for park facilities such as campsites and picnic pavilions and sought to boost revenue by establishing three state ski areas. Small local park systems keenly felt the paralyzing effects of reduced tax support, but the new York County Parks department was undeterred in its quest for development funds. During this period, York County, in the early development stages, was steward of thirty-four hundred acres of land, which were operated by a crew of nine men. Dauphin County, directly to the north, had seven hundred acres of county parkland and a crew of seven.

William A. Ehrman, a recent college graduate and the first Parks Director, bemoaned the loss of Housing and Urban Development money available through the Open Space Program, the termination of Project 70, and the exhaustion of Project 500 money. By 1975, the only remaining federal funds were Land and Water Conservation funds available through the Bureau of Outdoor Recreation, and those awards were exceedingly competitive as were the limited number of workers. The five-year average York County Parks budget of $267,000 left little for development of the system. County budgets—lacking federal money, state grants, or subsidies—were stretched to the limit. Increasing state-mandated county administrative costs for courts and human services left the parks out in the cold. There were no financial reservoirs for hard-pressed County Commissioners to dredge for the parks department, and County Commissioners were unwilling to risk the ire of taxpayers by increasing taxes, which were, nearly always, perceived by the public as excessive.

The hard reality left York County Parks trolling for ideas and led to one of the few public relations miscalculations ever made by the department. In 1975, in an effort to generate a self-supporting revenue resource in keeping with what was to become the federal injunction of James Watt, Secretary of the Interior under Ronald Reagan, to "make do with what you have," young

Ehrman recommended the board approve a feasibility study to evaluate the revenue potential of a public golf course in John Rudy County Park. He encouraged the board to consider the study since it was to be underwritten by the National Golf Council. Ehrman's particular means of securing an ongoing revenue source, such as a golf course, for the Parks system was well-intentioned but ill-advised.

When the press reported the prospect of using tax dollars for what was estimated to be a half-million-dollar public golf course in the county, which at the time had sixteen golf courses, the public response was swift and clear. Neil McGeehan, operator of the Yorktowne Golf Club, complained in a March 30, 1975, *Sunday News* article by Stew Mihm, "We have more public golf courses here than Philadelphia and Baltimore. Golfers can tee off within fifteen minutes compared to two-hour waits in Metropolitan areas … and golf is not a year-round activity in York County." Public voices of dissent were equally adverse. In a March 14, 1975, *Daily Record* account, Lore Spangenthal said, "I don't think golf courses should be built with taxpayer money. That is for private enterprise." Stan Hoke remarked, "There must be better uses for the money." Rosie Siltzer said, "I am not in favor. I don't play golf. Why a golf course? Why not something for everyone?" At the next board meeting, Sylvia Newcombe raised the question of how "unbiased" a golf course study by the National Golf Council would be. Joe Raab wisely questioned the financial solvency of golf course operations. In any event, as questions continued to surface, Raab and Newcombe found accord with their fellow board members and wasted no time tabling the golf course study. The subject was never broached again, leading to the obvious conclusion that the golf course notion was tabled six feet beneath the table.[31]

As discussions of the golf course circulated throughout the county, it was clear the people of York County wanted parks developed for broad segments of the public and not exclusive enclaves of special interests. The board did not mistake the message and illustrated its intention to serve the broadest public interest of the people of York County.

Chastened, but undiminished in his efforts, Ehrman continued to seek financial stability for the infant parks department. Soon after the golf course episode, he succeeded in persuading the board to create a revenue resource taskforce for the hardscrabble department, which it did.

Even though advances in parks and recreation within the second decade (1978–1988) were constrained by limited budgets, it was the greatest period of park development. The few remaining federal and state grants were spread out to develop portions of Rocky Ridge County Park and John Rudy County Park. An animal activity area at Spring Valley County Park was established, and facilities for the nature center were completed. The bridges along the Rail

Trail, destroyed by Hurricane Agnes in 1972, were funded. William Kain County Park received development assistance. Nonetheless, much was left to do, but there was no money. The "make do" spirit of the board and staff provided the impetus that attracted an unusual outpouring of community help. It would be impossible to enumerate all of the groups and individuals who have aided in the development of the parks, but a few examples illustrate the extent of community response.

Led by board member Tom Clough, a youth board gained community recognition for the parks by sponsoring and participating in environmental cleanups throughout the county.

York College undertook a study to consider ways of implementing volunteer park patrols to assist in rules enforcement.

The Rehabilitation and Industrial Training Center began training special needs citizens to participate in revenue generating programs at Spring Valley County Park, showcasing the links between agriculture and industry in York County. Among the programs RITC sought to encourage, in alliance with the parks, was the significance of milling in the community. Cross Mill was inventoried, and oral histories were obtained from the miller, Harry Cross, by RITC staff. Basketmaking was taught to provide examples of cornhusk baskets used to transport eggs, produce, and goods from field to market. Early on, the abundant yields of county farms made York a distribution hub, ultimately conveying locally produced goods throughout the nation in locally produced containers. Baskets were the forerunners of York's thriving container box industry.

The Louis Resser family helped RITC students plant and harvest broom corn at Spring Valley County Park to fabricate brooms illustrative of the agricultural heritage. Naylor Wineries offered native grapes for propagation in the heritage area of Spring Valley County Park for the folk life center.

To support the development of Spring Valley County Park and reflect the agricultural underpinnings of the industrial growth of York County, a prominent local artist, Othmar Carli, produced a limited edition print illustrating the evolution of York County from agriculture to industry to benefit the park.

The Folk Heritage Institute, led by Mark Motich, Ruth Davis Morse, and Karen Hostetter, scheduled seminars and folk music concerts in the park to benefit Spring Valley County Park. They collected oral histories documenting York's agricultural past and industrial origins centering around Spring Valley County Park and its environs. The histories were put in the care of Robert Terry, a professor in the York College of Pennsylvania History Department.

Despite the fact that Spring Valley County Park was the ideal location to showcase the link between agriculture and industry in York County, the idea was co-opted by like-minded individuals who sought to bring the genesis of industry to life in York city rather than the rustic fields of Spring Valley County Park. Nonetheless, utilization of the original Spring Valley County Park master plan to establish Spring Valley as a place for agricultural demonstrations of early farming techniques and manufacturing innovations in a natural setting remains a viable plan. Knowledge of the cultural heritage of a community is a keen drawing card for young and old. Joining forces to extend the reach of history into a natural setting seems an excellent basis for a natural alliance between the York County Parks and the York County Agricultural and Industrial Museum. The industrial museum in the urban setting of York city would be complemented by the agricultural antecedents best found in a rural agricultural venue such as Spring Valley County Park.

Park development was aided by the help and cooperation of community organizations together with a steadily growing stream of volunteers. The Audubon Society provided assistance to the Richard M. Nixon County Park, which led to its development as an environmental education showplace. Construction hurdles were overcome when Duane Close, Park Director and later board president, recounted the suggestion of his wife to the board. Eileen Close, a substitute teacher at York County Vocational Technical School, recommended involving students in a supervised project at the nature center at Nixon County Park to provide worthwhile work experiences for the students, which would also be a means of saving labor costs. The suggestion was welcomed, and the park's staff united with students from the York County Vocational Technical School to build the nature center. The plan followed a "green" construction design that is heralded as a model of energy efficiency. The combined efforts of the school and park staff are estimated to have reduced labor cost by half.

Nixon Nature Center during construction

Concrete surfaced Braille trails were installed by volunteers with locally donated materials at Nixon County Park. Together with Eagle Scouts, the park naturalist worked on stream reclamation. A wildlife census, conducted by the naturalist and volunteers, documented flora and fauna in the parks.

The staff enthusiastically labored to further the original aims of park development, but no means of generating substantial income for the parks had surfaced until the seed of an idea was sown in 1981 by Parks Director Guy Walker. Walker's idea proved to be a valuable revenue resource with broad public appeal. Walker promoted a Halloween haunted trail at Rocky Ridge County Park. The haunted trail was well attended and generated revenue for the parks. The department was in for a surprise when it did succeed in generating support on its own. Money raised by county departments is deposited in the County of York General Fund, which means it can be dispersed at the discretion of the County Commissioners and may or may not be returned to the department generating the income. As the board gained an understanding of the power of the county purse, they sought to avoid the vagaries of budget allocations.

In order to have the means at their disposal of self-supporting funds raised within the parks system, the board established the York County Parks Foundation Charitable Trust. In this way, money generated within the parks is insulated from the general fund and is directly available for park use. The trust is a way for any citizen to become a philanthropist. Planned estate giving for parks has appealed to many citizens. Donors forge a strong parks bond and identify themselves as the Gathering Leaves Society. Revenue from the trust shows steady annual growth.

logo

The Parks Board continues to implement self-supporting projects to defray park operation and development expenses. The department demonstrates its integrity by having never yielded to pressure to subvert its mission:

> *York County Department of Parks and Recreation enhances the quality of community life acting as a steward for the environment. In this capacity, it acquires, conserves and manages parklands and it offers a variety of recreational and educational opportunities.*

The mission statement reflects the philosophy of Udall, Goddard, Muir, and other farsighted leaders in the field; none of whom sought to exploit the role of park stewardship in a commercial way or to abandon the pledge to preserve natural land for future generations. Public land in the county of York is treasured. As federally owned public land was subjected to cries for oil drilling, the harvest of ancient timber, the development of casinos, or "revenue resourceful" endeavors, the York County Parks Board looked to its citizens, who have always participated in community efforts to supplement limited budgets and develop parks in accordance with its more conservative mission statement. Avoiding pressure to exploit parkland is primary. This approach has been extremely successful. Up to the present, the Parks Board continues to seek community support and is liberal in acknowledging participation by groups and individuals. Public involvement in park development is publicly acknowledged and appreciated. Board records cite countless contributions.

Parks Board meetings are open to the public and conducted with collegial decorum. At the height of the extremely active development period of the parks, the Nixon Environmental Education task force was acknowledged for its outstanding role. Members were seasoned organizers and planners. They were widely praised for their efforts, sparking renewed energy among the group for future park development. The Nixon County Park task force (chaired by Thomas Clough, a high school science teacher; Dr. Robert Denoncourt, York College of Pennsylvania; Hon. George Goodling, Member, U.S. Congress, 19th District; Shirley Shipley, Junior League; and John Smith, York County Agricultural Agent) were typical of members of the public who worked for the betterment of the parks and were called before the Parks Board to receive the only thing the parks have to give, grateful thanks for their support. William Koller also came before the board to be acknowledged for his generous gift of animal specimens that became the core of the addition to the Nixon County Park Environmental Education Center; and Dr. Kenneth Orwig, an entomologist, received thanks for the donation of his vast insect collection to the Environmental Center. Members of youth organizations were thanked.

4-H riding clubs, led by Anne Wagner, and the local affiliate of the United States Pony Club, the Old Rose Tree Pony Club, were acknowledged for contributions of cash and in-kind to the animal activity area in Spring Valley County Park.

During this period, Rev. Carroll C. Luckenbaugh chaired meetings of the congenial board with quiet dignity and a gentle manner. Minutes of meetings during the development phase of the parks are filled with difficulties the board faced and diligently strove to overcome. Members approached each problem with equanimity, always welcoming members of the public to meetings. As they discussed problems, they were often able to elicit helpful responses from attendees who were interested in the tireless work of York County Parks staff and the board. Public attendance at board meetings proved to be an excellent means of gaining support for the parks.

Unlike most visitors to board meetings, one posed a challenge to Luckenbaugh's patience. It was an aggrieved member of the public who lived near Rocky Ridge County Park and became a staple at board meetings. At first, during time allocated for the public to address the board, he waxed on, endlessly expressing his concerns among which was his desire for the hours of Rocky Ridge County Park to be unrestricted. He requested the park to be open twenty-four hours a day, seven days a week. He spoke of his opposition to hunting in the park and complained about the management of Rocky Ridge County Park. Board members politely attended his rambling discourses and repeatedly asked him to submit any and all of his requests in writing in order that they could be added to the already bulging agenda. No written requests were ever submitted, but the garrulous fellow continued to show up for every Parks Board meeting for a couple of years, speaking out whether recognized or not. When asked why he would not submit written proposals or requests about park hours or hunting regulations, he explained he was working "under cover" for a Washington agency supported by Common Cause.

The board tolerated the peculiar antics until an incident at Rocky Ridge County Park became the final straw. He approached two ladies hiking happily along a trail in Rocky Ridge County Park and evicted them from the park, declaring they would be arrested and fined if they violated park regulations again. The two hikers left and proceeded directly to the administrative headquarters of the Parks Department. They wanted to know what park regulation prevented them from enjoying a walk along a park trail. It didn't take much detective work to conclude the incident was the work of the habitual board visitor. When asked if he had evicted the ladies, he acknowledged he had. The board took long-overdue action. Luckenbaugh, the kindly chairman, advised him in no uncertain terms to desist in representing himself as a park law enforcement officer or he would be accountable to the law. The press relished making a story of the peculiar antics. Following the Rocky Ridge County Park incident, there is no record of board attendance by the aggrieved undercover agent. Board meetings during this stressful period of growth and development are unparalleled examples of grace under pressure by the chair and members of the board.[32]

The physical development of York County parks was essential, but so too was the development of park guardians, the rangers. Board member Jim Rebert, chair of the Law Enforcement Task Force, undertook a mission to secure better radio communication for park rangers who traveled alone on patrol throughout the parks late at night. A K-9 member of the force, Shadow, was enlisted to accompany the rangers. But one of the most difficult issues facing the department centered around armed patrols. Park rangers received Pennsylvania State Police training at the State Academy and were taught CPR, but they were not permitted to bear arms. Most incidents in the parks are nonconfrontational, such as walking a dog off leash or littering, but as the park system experienced greater use, more and more ominous reports of drunken parties, illegal hunting, and vandalism added a high degree of risk for unarmed rangers.

The position of the County Commissioners was for rangers to report incidents to local police departments for backup assistance. This was not effective since most encounters would escalate before a ranger could make a report, and violators would be long gone before a police department could respond. The resolution of the problem would continue into the third decade. Until then, rangers were essentially viewed as goodwill ambassadors lacking authority to enforce rules and regulations. This was regrettable because the state legislature had enacted legislation enabling park rangers to serve as enforcement agents in parks. Without self-protection while enforcing park regulations in potentially dangerous situations, unarmed rangers were in a double bind. It was particularly difficult during this period of rapid population growth in the county and resulted in as many as a thousand incident reports a month by the rangers.

The rangers held their own under the circumstances and worked diligently, as did each member of the park team. Austerity also did not stop the in-house maintenance crew. Construction of a sledding hill, rifle range, picnic pavilions, and hiking and riding trails were incorporated into their day-to-day maintenance work. Community-sponsored Arts in the Parks, horse shows, and archery competitions took hold, as well as community garden plots. The rapidly disappearing federal and state money was employed to establish soccer fields, softball fields, tennis courts, and picnic pavilions at John Rudy County Park. Remaining federal and state revenue was used to develop the Spring Valley County Park animal activity area and the folk life house.

Throughout this period, perhaps the only questionable use of funds was a "natural composting privy" in Spring Valley County Park. It was included in engineering drawings by Al Wright of Buchart Horn. When news reports of the $28,000 outhouse surfaced, plans for other natural composting potties in Spring Valley County Park were scrapped. Further arguments for armed rangers were strengthened when the one Spring Valley County Park natural composting potty was continuously vandalized until it was, finally, damaged beyond repair. By 2008, only one natural composting toilet, predating the Spring Valley County Park model, remains. It is located in a less vandal-prone spot at Lake Williams. There are portable toilets in some parks; all other park facilities have flush toilets.

Enhanced by the variety of parks springing to life in the county throughout the second decade, public attendance burgeoned, and community support soared as a result of the countless opportunities afforded by inviting county parks.

There had been some mistakes: golf courses and toilets; some regrets: the loss of the opportunity to save the Anderson house; some unusual experiences: antics at board meetings by the peculiar neighbor; unanticipated change: Cross Mill would not be relocated to Spring Valley County Park; but overall, the achievements of the staff, board, and public had resulted in an operational parks system. Parks were being used, and the environment of the parks was having the desired effect. People were responding to the nature and beauty of the parks and being uplifted. Members of the rapidly expanding population were enjoying the benefits of the York County Parks as potato fields began to sprout houses.

Chapter 4

1988–1997: Public Enjoyment

o o o o o o o o o o o o o o o o o o o o o o o o o o o o o o o o o o o o

The stimulation among all people of environmental awareness may, in the long run, prove to be the highest function of a Park System. In effect, it gathers together all the cultural, historic and natural strands of the System to make man aware of his priceless heritage and his own environmental responsibilities to it.

Stewart Udall,
United States Secretary of the Interior

In 1988, at the outset of its third decade, York County Parks was custodian of over thirty-seven hundred acres. Farms, forests, fields, and lakes were being transformed into welcoming havens for increasing numbers of citizens, drawn as by magnets to delight in the natural settings that afforded increasing opportunities for active and passive recreation and relaxation. Throughout the previous decades, the board and staff were occupied with acquisition and development of parkland. Now the emphasis was directed toward maintenance. The staff had increased from one in 1968 to forty-eight full-time employees in 1996 before budget cutbacks. The parks budget had increased to just under $600,000.

Acquisition and development continued, but it was seldom bolstered by state or federal funds. Private donations were a growing source of support for the success of the parks. Community groups and individuals assisted the staff in enhancing facilities, services, and programs.

In 1993, a twenty-eight-acre parcel of what once had been 170 thriving iron ore mines in York County during the mid-nineteenth century was given to York County for a park by a waste management company, Modern Landfill and Recycling. In 1997, an additional forty-five acres was added to the original gift, increasing the park size to seventy-three acres. The new park was named P. Joseph Raab County Park in tribute to the inspired foresight and leadership of the parks' founder. The old mine shafts scattered throughout the park are havens for exceptional bat populations—little brown bats, big brown bats, northern long-eared bats, and eastern pipistrelle bats. The old mines provide an ideal habitat. In addition to hiking paths throughout the park, there are staff-guided archaeological and nature explorations for adventure seekers and scientists. Development of a park requires full staff support. There are countless responsibilities attendant to operating any public park. When the P. Joseph Raab County Park joined the system, the endless "to-do" list of the small York staff took on added tasks of securing the mines, clearing trails, wildlife surveys, public information, education, press releases, parking areas, signs for entrances, trails, rest areas, and the demarcation of boundaries. All were put in place by the stalwart staff.

During this period, a retired contractor, William G. Koller, came forward to offer the department 170 wildlife specimens he had acquired on hunting expeditions throughout the world. Parks Naturalist Francis Velazquez, who joined the staff in 1984, recalls an invitation from Mr. Koller to view the collection. Velazquez said the day was icy and snow was falling, but he enlisted Park Superintendent William McCue to give him a lift to the Kollers' home in a four-wheel-drive county vehicle. The two men stomped the snow from their boots and entered the house to what Velazquez characterizes as an "incredible" sight. Imposing figures of animals occupied nearly every space. Beautifully mounted museum quality specimens returned the stares of the two men. The house was a veritable museum.

William and Gladys Koller at home with his trophies.

There was no question as to the desirability of the collection, but there was a hitch. Koller said his contribution hinged on the county agreeing to construct a suitable exhibition hall for the mounts at Richard M. Nixon County Park within a reasonable time. As McCue and Velazquez departed from what Velazquez maintains was one of his most memorable park experiences, he asked the generous donor for an explanation of what had motivated him to part with his trophies. The sprightly old gentleman nodded with a smile and upon brief reflection said his wife had a growing collection of her own: porcelain, ceramic, and bronze poultry figurines. He chuckled and allowed he was just accommodating his wife and making room in the house for the chickens. The priceless collection was accepted by the County Commissioners with gratitude, but keeping the promise to construct what became known as the Treasury of Wildlife Wing became no small problem. The solution was, of course, left to York County Parks.

The County Commissioners did allocate a small amount from a bond issue, but it was far from sufficient to complete the project. Fundraising groups were engaged and public relations avenues explored. A public relations firm headquartered in Tennessee, Holliman Associates, assisted in developing a strategy. During the construction phase, in-house solicitations for small paid Environmental Center memberships, led by Parks Naturalist Kim Young, greatly assisted fundraising and broadened community awareness. Major donations were solicited under the guidance of Luther Sowers,[33] who ran with the ball. Charles Falkler, Chairman of the Parks Board, enlisted Sowers, a popular retired school superintendent and native son, to preside over the York County Parks Foundation Charitable Trust, which, in turn, led to his chairmanship of the capital campaign for the Koller collection. Robert Kinsley, the contractor for the project, worked on faith and finished the project, which was dedicated in 1992. The Treasury of Wildlife Wing was enjoyed by the public for a couple of years before Kinsley received final payment for his work in December 1994. Mr. Koller was well-advised to extract a promise of *reasonable time* for completion of the project in view of what occurred with Wallace-Cross Mill.

Early in 1986, the Spring Valley County Park Task Force, in collaboration with C. S. Davidson, developed a master plan that was submitted for approval in 1987. It is the most comprehensive county park plan on record. The plan was not adopted by the York County Commissioners until 1990. Included in the park development were provisions for the relocation of Cross Mill to one of seven millsites in Spring Valley County Park. The configuration of the overshot waterwheel of the old mill fit the dimensions of one of the existing park millraces perfectly.

Wallace Cross Mill before restoration

The mill was given to the parks in 1978 and had operated until a few years before Harry Cross died Christmas 1987. When Cross died, a series of events resulted in a legal dispute with Russell Trout, Cross's nephew, who bought the thirteen-acre Cross estate at auction and laid claim to the mill. The author, a neighbor of Cross who had encouraged him to donate the mill to York County Parks during her tenure as a Parks Board member, championed the battle for the mill. The basis of the dispute centered around an agreement that the county solicitor, Louis Sterling, prepared at the time of the donation of the mill to the county. The agreement gave Harry Cross a life estate in the property, with sole authority to maintain and run the mill with assistance from the Parks Department only by his request. Regrettably, there was no provision for maintenance of the mill in the event Harry Cross was incapable of administering the mill, which is exactly what happened. When Cross's health failed and he required nursing home care, the mill was left in limbo for a number of years. No authority existed for anyone to take over operation or maintainence of the mill.

The York County Commissioners determined the deteriorating old mill was inconsequential to the county and, outside the bounds of the sunshine law, considered giving title to the mill to private individuals for a fishing camp. The plan sprung a leak when word reached the author. Cross Mill is indisputably the most generous gift ever made to York County. It represented the bulk of Harry Cross's estate. He was encouraged to make the donation by the author who believed the county would be the most secure custodian of his mill. Neither Cross or the author were aware that gifts to government entities do not guarantee perpetual care, and gifts once given are subject to disposal. Cross gave careful thought to his decision for several years before legally cementing his gift to the people of York County for what he thought would be all time. When asked if he had considered giving the mill to his children, he said he would never wish the work the mill represented on his children. He hoped their lives would not be as hard as his had been. He did want the mill legacy to live on, however, and vested his trust in York County to preserve this piece of living history, one of few, if not the only, small custom water-powered grist mills remaining in operation in all of the Commonwealth.[34]

The lesson that governments are at liberty to dispose of assets as they deem fit was a hard-learned lesson. Conscience-stricken that the mill was about to be disposed of by the county, the author attended the final Wednesday meeting of the outgoing Board of Commissioners in December, and during the period reserved for the public to address the board, inquired about the status of the mill, raising the curtain on what would become a testy legal dispute. The Commissioners responded to the inquiry with a question. They asked who would be remotely interested in the old mill, how much restoration would be, and what source of money to preserve it was available. In response the author proposed that it would require as much as $100,000 to put the mill in shape, and the community would stand behind the effort. The outgoing board deferred to a request by incoming County Commissioner George Trout, who appealed the decision to dispose of the mill until a test of community interest could assess what financial assistance might be available. Outgoing County Commissioner Lorraine Hovis granted a ninety-day extension for the author to seek community support.

During the grace period, appeals to organizations and individuals throughout the county were made. Among the first to endorse the effort was mill authority Stephen Kendig, who himself lives in a mill in Oley, Pennsylvania. Kendig was born and reared in York County to a family long known for its love of history. He offered his support so long as the mill *not* be removed from its original site. He explained that moving the mill would compromise its historic integrity. The Red Lion and Stewartstown Historical Societies, Historic York, Inc., The Society for the Preservation of Old Mills, feed companies, engineers, architects, and countless history buffs joined forces. An industrialist, Harvey Bradley, CEO of Bradley Lifting Company, was among the first to add considerable weight to the preservation defense. He offered to restore the Fitz waterwheel at his York plant.[35] In addition, he enlisted Ray Boasman to replicate the ten-foot wooden screw employed to hoist the stones in the mill for dressing, which had gone missing during the period Harry Cross was in a nursing home. During that period, many priceless mill artifacts disappeared even before the public auction.

Mrs. Shoemaker's Weybright Hounds, the author's pack, sponsored a well-publicized "Been Through the Mill Weekend," with all proceeds going to the mill. The activities included a full-dress Hunt Ball at the Red Lion Country Club on the Friday evening of the weekend. Saturday, not far from the mill, the foxhounds were cast for a formal fox chase. Hounds were followed by a liveried group of adults and children mounted on handsome steeds. Spectators, characterized as "hill toppers" in foxhunting nomenclature, lined the fields, watching what was for many a first. The fox chase was followed by a breakfast at the Glen Rock Mill Inn, where festive music and dancing enhanced by a well laid table of traditional fare served following hunts. On Sunday, a foot hunt with Elizabeth Streeter's Chester County French Basset Hounds pursuing cottontail rabbits was followed by a tea at Mackley's Mill in Hellam to conclude the weekend. Following basset hounds, whose bellies nearly touch the ground, is preferred by sports enthusiasts who enjoy a pleasant day walking across hill and dale rather than the frenetic pace of mounted sport. Few of the attendees had experienced chasing sports, and most were delighted to learn that basset hounds have little inclination to do the bunny harm. The enjoyment is finding the scent of a rabbit and giving voice in their mournful baritone chorus as they and the foot followers meander, at a basset pace, on the line of the scent.

By the end of the fun-filled weekend, pledges in kind and cash of nearly $100,000 were secured—convincing proof for the new Board of Commissioners that the mill did warrant being saved. That, however, did not resolve the legal dispute with Russell Trout, who continued to claim title to the mill. It was not until 1996 that the mill and slightly over one acre of ground was deeded to the county, resolving the dispute once and for all. It was eighteen years after Harry Cross gave his mill to the county and nearly ten years from the time of his death. The money from the fund drive was placed in custody of Historic York, Inc., where it drew interest until it was put to use in the restoration.[36]

Harry Cross filling the mill hopper

A committee worked diligently to restore the mill and have it designated a historic site, the first of many historic sites to be administered by York County Parks. The mill would in time become a park in its own right. Putting the mill in working shape was one of the first of many challenges Tom Brant faced when he assumed directorship of York County Parks in December 1994. Much of the restoration was done by the parks' maintenance staff. Joe Z, a local tinsmith, faithfully recreated the original standing seam tin roof; Bradley and Boasman spent endless hours working on the mechanical elements. The staff stained, sealed, painted, and repaired the old mill. Francis Velazquez designed and created educational exhibits. Meetings with Labor and Industry took staff time. A mill history was composed, and a scrapbook filled with interesting accounts of the mill was created.

During the same year, the County Commissioners turned over maintenance and development of the ninety-two county-owned bridges to York County Parks. The demands on the staff were, to say the least, burdensome. As revenues dwindled, the staff sought means to combine park activities into a low-cost big-dollar revenue resource.

Among the income-producing resources for York County Parks, memberships at Nixon County Park, boat rental income, vending machines, and special events were helpful, but none generated much supplemental income. The Halloween Haunted Trail Guy Walker began in the early 1980s was phased out in 1994 and succeeded by a successful annual light show, "Christmas Magic—A Festival of Lights." On Walker's recommendation, the board inaugurated the light show at Rocky Ridge Park during the Christmas season. The concept of a light show was propitious. It employed park personnel to good advantage during a downturn in park activity and brought visitors into the park during an off-season. Since its inception, Christmas Magic has become a "must-see" regional event, drawing over 589,000 visitors through 2008. In 2006 the *Philadelphia Inquirer* cited Christmas Magic as one of the top ten Christmas events in Pennsylvania. Earlier, in 2003, the *Wall Street Journal* named Christmas Magic one of the top thirteen holiday events in the United States. Best of all, the modest admission fee to Christmas Magic is a tremendous boon to York County Parks coffers.

Christmas Magic at Rocky Ridge Park

By 2008, the event receipts totaled $148,630. Since preparations occur during downturns in park usage, staff and a growing number of volunteers are able to expand the event each year. What began as festive strings of colorful Christmas lights laid along the ground from tree to tree has become a sophisticated trail with an underground electrical system running throughout the park. The entire electrical system was installed by the York County Parks maintenance crew. The lights of Christmas Magic, visible for miles, brightly illuminate the hillside of Rocky Ridge County Park throughout the holiday season. The event attracts thousands to follow the path of lights. Attendance figures increase each year as if to match the bright lights of the expanding displays.

In 1994, Guy Walker submitted his resignation. The department operated without a director for several months until Tom Brant assumed the role in December 1994. Brant came aboard with a boatload of existing projects awaiting attention and an unusual new one.

In the early 1970s, York County Parks supported a new park concept, linear parks. Though York County stood in the vanguard with its early endorsement of the concept, little had happened until 1990. The unlikely beginnings of the park were rooted in the nineteenth century, when the United States embarked on the greatest railroad-building spree in history. By 1916, the country boasted the largest railroad system in the world, having nearly 300,000 miles of track connecting the smallest towns to the largest cities.[37] But the rise of cars, trucks, buses, and air transportation contributed to an equally rapid decline of railroads. There were no visionaries to anticipate an oil-dependent nation suffering regret over the loss of nearly half of the original

United States rail system and the relatively inexpensive travel afforded by rail transportation. The decline of railroads coincided with a growing movement for public foot trails.

Early signs of yearning for a return to nature as the country, no longer largely agricultural, was transformed into an urban population can be traced to 1936, the year the Appalachian Trail running from Maine to Georgia began. Boosted by the rise of the environmental movement in the 1960s, interest in rail trails picked up added steam and received a major lift in 1968 with the adoption of the National Trail Systems Act. A system of twenty-three thousand miles of nationally designated scenic and historic trails was authorized by the act. Other federal legislative support for rail trails came in the 1980s and 1990s. In 1983 Congress amended the National Trail Systems Act to permit the preservation of abandoned rail corridors for future trail use through a process known as "rail banking." In 1991 Congress acted again, to establish the Intermodal Surface Transportation Efficiency Act (ISTEA), which made more than $350 million available for rail-trail projects; and in 1998 Congressional support continued with an expanded Transportation Equity Act for the 21st Century (TEA-21). Thousands of communities began reclaiming abandoned rail corridors as public trails for commuters, walkers, joggers, bicyclists, horseback riders, individuals with disabilities, and others. A national Rails-to-Trails Conservancy was founded in 1985, at which time there were seventy-five rail trails in the United States. By 1992 the number had exploded to five hundred. In 1998 another twelve hundred rail-trail projects, involving nearly nineteen thousand miles, were on the drawing boards, and York County was among them. In 1998 there were one thousand rail trails scattered throughout the United States, a network of rail trails roughly equivalent to a quarter of the length of the United States interstate highway system.

In March 1990 the York County Commissioners put a Rail Trail Authority in place, empowering what had, until that time, been an informal parks task force. The authority was granted the right to plan and seek funds to develop the old Penn Central double-bed track into a recreational corridor. Tammy Klunk, who joined York County Parks in 1982 as Assistant Program Coordinator, was assigned to assist the new group. She was the sole staff support for the authority, a Herculean task added to her numerous other, no less demanding, job responsibilities. Her recollection of the first meeting of the Rail Trail Authority gave her pause. The meeting was called to order in the fourth-floor County Commissioners' meeting room in the old courthouse. The room was filled to capacity with indignant people. Tim Fulton chaired the meeting and skillfully guided members of the authority. He was adept at responding with equanimity to the hostile citizens, present for the sole purpose of expressing opposition to the rail trail. It took two years for the public to be won over to the benefits of a recreational corridor. A large part of the reversal of public opinion can be credited to Fulton's artful public relations skills.

Tim Fulton first chairman of the York County Heritage Rail Trail Authority

Authority meetings were no longer fraught with bitter members of the public, but by a growing group of admirers who looked forward to the benefits of a linear park. Most visceral opponents of the project had been adjacent landowners of the rail line. Their fears had to be rendered groundless in order for the rail trail to prevail. To that end, the resolve of the authority never waned. When the landowners were placated, outreach for broad public support began. It was complicated. Eleven municipalities were involved. Rights to lay underground utilities had to be secured from each government entity. Bridges washed out in 1972 by Hurricane Agnes required reconstruction, which involved structural engineers and labor. Historic sites along the route required inventories and submission of each site for inclusion on the appropriate Historic Register and budgets for costly restorations. A suitable multiuse surface to meet the requirements of various users had to be determined. Hikers, runners, bicyclists, horseback riders, and wheelchair users would all expect to enjoy the trail. The initial project required assembly of a crew to clear the first mile of track from the Maryland line to New Freedom. Tammy Klunk was involved each step of the way. She helped clear the trail, met with officials, kept records, attended meetings, wrote press releases, and was finally able to report to the authority that a $1.3 million grant she had submitted to the Pennsylvania Transportation Department had been approved. The Department of Conservation and Natural Resources (DCNR) matched money raised in a locally led capital fund campaign, and the rail trail was gradually transformed from a plan to a reality.

In 1991, York County Parks was able to reduce paperwork and enter the computer age, thanks to the gift of a computer from York Waste Disposal, Inc., and a printer from the People's Bank of Glen Rock. The maintenance department constructed a workstation for the electronic marvels. Staff training brought the office team up to speed as they entered the paperless age of accounting and record keeping. The efficiency of computerized scheduling was a boon to the department, saving countless hours of painstaking labor. The benefit of a small, overworked county department becoming computerized is hard to measure but unquestionably profound.

Activities in the parks were growing rapidly, but staff support was static until 1996, when the staff took a hard hit; staffing levels were again decreased in 2003. Their numbers were reduced from forty-eight to thirty-two. By 2008 the staff numbered even fewer—thirty.

Over the years, supplemental help was available from time to time from the York County Prison Outmate Program and a "catch-as-catch-can" series of interns from the York College Recreation Department under the direction of then-department chair, Annette Logan, a staunch supporter of York County Parks, and subsequent department chairs. Many staff members have joined the ranks of York County Parks as a result of Logan's influence and her support of the system. Help also surfaced from the alphabet soup of state-funded job training programs: CETA, PCC, and JTPA. Though the help was generally seasonal, it was always welcome.

Attempts to deal with labor shortages created interesting dilemmas. One, curiously, a volunteer effort to bring attention to Earth Day sponsored by an elementary school class accompanied by adult volunteers, involved picking up trash for a few hours in Spring Valley County Park. The seemingly good deed resulted in an incident with the county employee union. Union workers, appealing for more work hours and better pay, objected to the cleanup day, asserting it eliminated hours of employment for them. The cleanup was conducted by the class, but the issue surfaced again, this time from another perspective.

Volunteer members of the Spring Valley County Park task force, including respected 4-H leaders Anthony Dobrosky and the husband-wife team of Anne and Jack Wagner, led a campaign to add a second large exhibition ring and watering system to the animal activity area. As the center attracted more users each year, a second ring was in demand.

An equestrian competition at the Spring Valley Park animal activities center

Absent county, state, or federal funds, the task force team raised nearly $30,000 from fund drives, donations, and individuals. They not only covered the cost of labor and materials—the group did most of the work. County Commissioner Lorraine Hovis went on record as being strongly opposed to the effort because, out of hundreds of hours of labor, it involved a total of ten hours of parks' staff time. The maintenance staff used the county auger to dig some of the postholes for the new ring. There is no record of any expression of thanks by the County Commissioners for the otherwise "no-cost" contribution to the animal activity area. In fact, Hovis admonished the parks' board to be more diligent in their oversight of what was going on in the parks and not allow the maintenance crew to participate in such activities. Also, no acknowledgment of the added revenue the new ring generated for York County Parks, or appreciation for the efforts of countless volunteers, has ever been noted. Thankfully, Dobrosky and the Wagners, as well as all the volunteer groups, were not seeking recognition in their efforts to maintain and improve the facilities. Perhaps it can be summarized as a good example of the well-worn cliché that no good deed goes unpunished.

Among outstanding staff programs, those at the Nixon Park Nature Center under Kim Young are near the top.

Kim Young at the Nature Center

Young, the chief naturalist, had a staff of two, which was reduced to one in 1989. Nonetheless, she implemented a wildlife rescue program at Nixon Park in 1988. The program was introduced as a wildlife rehabilitation workshop and attracted sixty interested volunteers. She assisted veterinarians with training volunteers in conjunction with the Pennsylvania Game Commission. The results of the work led to establishment of a place for injured wildlife to be treated and rejuvenated before returning to nature. A Red Lion veterinarian, Dr. Don Patton, DVM, expressed interest and dedicated untold hours of time to ensure the program's success. Later he gave freely of his time as a dedicated Parks Board member.

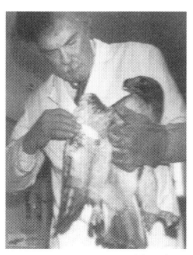

Dr. Don Patton DVM treating an injured hawk at the Nature Center

As a result of Young's work, she was named Conservationist of the Year by the Pennsylvania Federation of Sportsmen, York County Chapter, in 1988. At the outset of the Koller Treasury of Wildlife Wing fund drive, Young began a membership campaign for the Nature Center to aid the effort. By the end of 1989, results of the membership effort, together with gift shop sales, yielded a profit of $9,000. Another successful project during Kim Young's tenure was an annual bird-seed sale. Twenty-five percent of the income from the sale of bird seed was given to York Wildcare, and 75 percent was earmarked for the Nature Center. By 1990, over 1,800 people had attended York Wildcare bluebird workshops. A Reptile Weekend brought scores of curious visitors to the Nature Center to witness venom-milking demonstrations, observe reptiles, and learn the habits of slithering creatures. Children and parents gained respect and knowledge at the Nature Center obtainable in no other way in York County. Audubon Weekends, featuring special walks and lectures covering topics such as honeybees and wildflower identification; birding classes; and nature classes for children filled the Nature Center with growing numbers of new and old ardent nature devotees. The annual Dinosaur Weekend became another big draw for young and old.

Among other unsung efforts to Young's credit was an ongoing outreach to recruit and train volunteers to supplement the overworked, understaffed Nixon team. When she left in 1998, York County Parks was at the top of its game, benefiting from a skillfully executed environmental education center plan that continues to serve as a model of imagination and innovation. Young's legacy is invaluable. Duane Close's design has been emulated. During Young's tenure, Lancaster County used Nixon County Park as a model for its center, and Harford Glen Environmental Education Center of Maryland found the design of Nixon County Park to be the standard.

Longtime staff member Jeri Jones worked with Tammy Klunk organizing and promoting Arts in the Parks. Jones was instrumental in promoting instructed stargazing opportunities organized by Friends of the Observatory as public events. Another especially successful activity Jones introduced into park programs was gold panning at Spring Valley County Park. Delighted participants search mostly in vain, but leave the park filled with excitement about what they learned and the treasure they might discover on a future visit. Jones also created slide shows of trails and trail conduct to attract and inform hikers and fitness buffs.

Gold panning in the East Branch of the Codorus Creek at Spring Valley Park

In 1993, Jones took York County Parks on the road in a mobile unit that included a parks display and science lab. The rig was a donation from Hoss's Steak House. Jones toured schools throughout the county with the "Discovery Center," tempting teachers and students with bits and pieces of things to discover in the parks. The Discovery Center was decommissioned in 2000, when park attendance no longer required taking the message beyond park boundaries. By then, the people of York County were fully aware of the benefits to be discovered in the county parks.

The parks' maintenance staff resembles jacks-of-all-trades and masters of many. They lay stone, build fences, clear trails, construct picnic pavilions and tables, and add their "can-do" spirit to any and all park projects that need an extra hand.

One of the best public relations vehicles of York County Parks, apart from the parks themselves, is a newsletter, *Fox Tracks*, which Tammy Klunk organizes for publication. Salient articles of new development, volunteer achievements, funding, acquisitions, and activities drafted with journalistic skill are much anticipated publications.

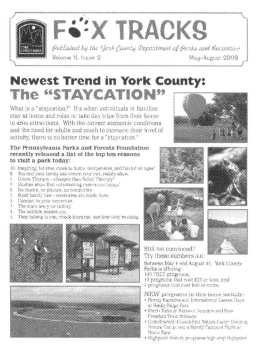

Fox Tracks, the Parks newsletter

Another in-house talent, Mike Fobes, designs, develops, edits, and produces park brochures and fliers.

Park rangers are traditionally viewed as public relations officers, but in a vast parks system, they are also called upon to enforce rules and regulations. This aspect of their work was in dispute for many years. The question of whether they should be armed was ongoing. Often, working alone, rangers encountered unruly drunken or drugged groups in the parks, and their recourse was to call 911 for local assistance. In reality, by the time backup support arrived on the scene, the offending rascals would be long gone, and the best outcome would be that the ranger had not been injured when he intervened in the illegal fun. Rangers also lead search-and-rescue missions in the parks and, on occasion, have the gruesome task of searching for missing persons suspected of being suicidal, only to, sadly, arrive too late.

Rangers are assigned at random throughout the park system since their ranks are insufficient to cover the entire system at all times. Their work is not always grim. Among some of the fun recollections is one occasion when the public was implicated in an old-fashioned prank. A busy event at Rocky Ridge County Park resulted in numerous calls to the rangers office with complaints about the ladies restroom being unavailable. A ranger arrived and found a "wet paint" sign at the entrance to the ladies' room. He called maintenance to inquire when the paint would be dry enough and learned the restroom had not been painted. The ranger was applauded by the long line of waiting ladies as he removed the sign.

Then there is the case of enforcement of park rules. In October 1993, a mother and her fifteen-year-old daughter were gathering leaves at Rocky Ridge Park for a biology assignment when they were apprehended by a hypervigilant ranger who politely informed them they were in violation of park regulations. "If everyone did what you are doing, there would be no leaves left in the park."[38] When approached, Guy Walker backed the ranger until a later time when a less tiresome view was taken of leaf thieves, and they were able to return to the park to gather leaves without fear of penalty or damaged reputations.

York County Park Rangers showing off their fleet

In January 1992, Pennsylvania Legislative Act 120 provided approval for park rangers to be trained to carry firearms. The York County rangers were enrolled at Harrisburg Area Community College for the official training and finally sent out on dark nights alone into tenuous situations but, at last, not without defensive protection. No incident has resulted from armed rangers, and there are, no doubt, many dangerous situations that have been diffused by knowledge that the rangers are able to enforce park regulations with impunity.

Potentially dangerous situations have been averted so far. An encounter by Ranger Scott Neely one night in 1991 occurred when he single-handedly disarmed a man at the Spring Valley County Park rifle range without incident. One shudders to imagine the result had the park visitor resisted. Neely recounts less alarming job experiences, such as helicopter surveys of park grounds for elusive crops of marijuana and scuba diving in Lake Williams to check on fish habitat, with far greater delight. Most rangers report high job satisfaction as a result of working with the largely law-abiding park visitors.

The highlight of the third parks decade was the assembly of one of the finest public staffs to be found. Requests from other parks departments for technical support in administration and management are fielded by the department with regularity. Recognition of the achievements of the small staff line the walls of the parks' office, but the greatest acknowledgment is found among the thousands of members of the public who are unceasing in their praise of the York County Parks. Director Tom Brant's transitions appeared effortless. He moved from meetings on environmental issues, to butterfly searches, to labor issues, threading his way through uncounted hours of work for York County Parks. His cool demeanor made the endless tasks appear effortless. Throughout his tenure, Brant supported the staff in outreach efforts to spur volunteer involvement in park activities. Brant's unique ability to sustain the impressive output of the department and the morale of a lean staff might be compared to a long-tailed cat moving through a room filled with rocking chairs—it's possible, but not easy.

Chapter 5
1998–2008: Public Support

o o o o o o o o o o o o o o o o o o o o o o o o o o o o o o o o o o o o o

Good, the more communicated, the more abundant grows.
John Milton
(1608–1674)

At the outset of the fourth decade, the staff, board, and ubiquitous volunteer corps of the York County Parks continued to collect accolades for outstanding work. Volunteers form an invaluable support network, and its success is no accident. Staff leadership and thoughtful management of volunteers developed incrementally, in part the unintended consequence of limited budgets. The department's outreach to volunteers evolved as the means to expand services. Volunteers provide an innovative solution to an age-old dilemma: are parks department funds to be used for conservation or recreation?

The department is charged with the acquisition, maintenance, and conservation of undisturbed natural environments for posterity, which appears to establish its essential role as stewardship. Park stewardship reflects the philosophy of the father of the national parks, John Muir, who espoused the ideal, "There should be no observable intrusion on pristine wilderness." Unaltered and untrammeled land was to be the aim. Given Muir's view, any alternative use of land had to conform to what is defined as *passive recreation*.[39] This philosophy is reflected in the mission statement of the department:

> *York County Department of Parks & Recreation enhances the quality of community life by acting as a steward for the environment. In this capacity it acquires, conserves, and*

manages parklands and offers a variety of recreational and educational opportunities.

This philosophy is in keeping with traditional funding streams for park "opportunities," which are usually designated for acquisition, capital improvements, and maintenance. Few dollars are allocated for educational programs, and fewer still for programmed recreation. Nonetheless, over the years, the department has provided recreation opportunities predicated on the criterion that there be no adverse effect on parkland. Conservation is the foremost consideration for parkland use.

Recommendations of the 2006 York County Open Space and Greenways Plan, a component of the York County Comprehensive Plan, authorize local municipalities to be agents of active community recreation. Many local municipalities fill the role successfully. Sometimes, however, limited space for active recreation in local municipalities results in appeals by municipalities to York County Parks for assistance. The availability of large county parks makes it possible in some circumstances to provide space for active recreation. Local needs can be met by calling upon the hidden weapon of the parks department, volunteers.

York County Parks is legally empowered to establish passive recreation areas in parks. Passive recreation areas preclude motorized activity, extensive physical alterations, and program funding. Areas established by the department are dependent on users to enliven them with activity: hiking, biking, horseback riding, picnicking, bird-watching, stargazing, canoeing, kayaking, and the plethora of activities that can only be fully enjoyed in natural settings. People bring the element of active recreation into natural park settings, reflecting the ideal espoused by Pennsylvania Governor Gifford Pinchot, "Public land should be preserved to produce the greatest good, for the greatest number, for the longest run."

Pinchot's objective was unlike John Muir's, which sought to preserve parks as exclusive, pristine enclaves for wildlife and nature. Pinchot did share Muir's goal of conservation, but he insisted conservation need not exclude people. Pinchot proclaimed that parks are for people.

The seemingly contradictory principles of conservation and recreation have been reconciled in the York County Parks system, and some *active* community recreation needs, otherwise lacking, are being met. A case in point is the township surrounding John Rudy County Park. It is a relatively densely populated residential area that lacked a suitable venue for athletic fields.

Township citizens petitioned York County Parks for athletic fields, which are regarded as active recreation areas. While acknowledging athletic fields as contrary to passive recreation goals (preserving undisturbed natural settings as places apart from congestion and noise), the board entertained the request. Encounters with nature are the highlight of natural environments. Pleasure is derived from the setting, not artificial embellishments such as fairgrounds, swimming pools, skating rinks, or soccer fields. The answer to the request lay in the park site in question, John Rudy County Park, since the request for athletic fields on that site was logical. The request was granted. The decision was based on sound reasoning. The location of the park, amid a heavily populated residential community, would, undeniably, attract large numbers of visitors from the surrounding neighborhoods, making retention of an undisturbed natural environment unlikely.

It was agreed that it would be preferable to provide a well-designed space for active, programmed activities for the growing numbers of young people in the area of the park, so long as compelling evidence of community support eliminating financial demands on York County Parks for staff was available. Budget resources to staff active recreation areas in county parks are nonexistent. Thus, with the clear understanding that York County Parks would provide the facility, not the staff, the athletic fields were approved for inclusion in the park master plan. Volunteers, not paid staff, would staff the athletic programs. There was consensus that low-impact recreation areas, such as athletic fields, in a small portion of the park would not detract from the park's natural beauty or adversely affect the area.

The example set in forging alliances between professional staff and volunteers has become the core of park success. York County Parks oversees the maintenance and conservation of parkland, and volunteers assist in implementing programs and activities. Using this model, York County Parks can respond to public requests for active recreation use in passive recreation areas as long as conservation criteria and operation costs are met. In general, programs or facilities come into existence in response to public requests. A group of volunteer advocates approach the board and outline their interest in an activity. When feasible, the department makes space for the activity within the guidelines of a park master plan. An area is made available by York County Parks, and a team of volunteers conducts programs under the auspices of York County Parks. Promulgation of wholesome activities is feasible due to volunteer involvement. Staffing predicated on volunteer commitment is more difficult than hiring personnel to facilitate programs. The parks' plan is successful because active recreation areas are put in place in response to community demand and come with a volunteer base to ensure community support from the outset.

Volunteers are the capstone of the York County Parks' success. Their efforts integrate recreational activities into overall park master plans in ways that are compatible with the basic goals of conservation.

Park volunteers hard at work on a park trail

The parks department fulfills its stewardship role, conserving and protecting the natural beauty, without forestalling the recreational interests of citizens. It is a win-win situation. Transparency in all the work of the department is the key. There are no deleterious effects on parkland in the present or the future. Public use of the parks is welcomed and encouraged. Development of passive recreation areas in the parks—such as trails, picnic areas, boats, garden plots, fishing, and space for parking—are incorporated into park master plans as part of the department mission. The volunteer corps cultivates responsible use of parkland by implementing and organizing activities and programs.

Master plans detail the natural features of a park, together with the history, scientific significance, records of developed sites, and community interests. Each master plan incorporates the results of surveys and public meetings, which reflect the needs and desires of the community.

One example of incremental implementation of a master plan is Spring Valley County Park. It contains seven millsites, a historic house, undulating hills, a wide variety of flora and fauna, streams, woods, and fields. It is an 867-acre park situated in what historically has been an agricultural area. Traditionally, residents in the area have kept livestock, ridden horses, and gathered for competitions and fellowship. Over the course of the past forty years, the area surrounding Spring Valley County Park has been in transition. Exurbanites, longing for quasicountry lives on a few acres, have joined the farm community. The newcomers shared the community interest in gathering places for family activities and recreation sites including animal activities. The master plan was responsive to the interest. Community volunteers supported the concept of a place for families to gather for dog trials, horse shows, livestock exhibitions, picnics, and trail rides in the midst of the beautiful unspoiled parkland. The use was compatible with the conservation aims of the master plan. The parks department provides the place; volunteers implement the activities.

Thoughtful land conservation planning requires vigilant attention to design. The site chosen for the animal activities area was done with an eye to the natural topography, with special consideration for drainage. Major earthmoving equipment was inappropriate and thereby unacceptable. The level site selected was open fields on the perimeter of the park. The site was the least intrusive on the natural setting. Accessibility is a major consideration for any project. The primary entry, two miles off an interstate exit, eliminated overuse of local roads or the necessity for new roads. The animal activities area was developed with some public funds, but a large part of the development monies came from contributions of time and money from community organizations. The Old Rose Tree Pony Club, a member club of the United States Pony Clubs; White Rose 4-H and several other local 4-H clubs; and Penn State Agricultural Extension, to name a few, made contributions. Anthony Dobrosky, retired Penn State Agricultural Extension Agent, worked tirelessly throughout development. Maintenance, scheduling, and terms of use for the center were established by the Parks Department. Programs at the animal activity area are planned and conducted by volunteers within the park guidelines.

Other similar programs, run by volunteers, flourish throughout the park system. The quid pro quo is a parks department meeting its overarching goal of preserving land for future generations and a community benefiting from volunteer-run recreational activities in spectacular locations. Another benefit is derived from modest user fees for events at the animal activities area and similar venues. The fees produce a small, ongoing revenue resource offsetting, to a small degree, maintenance cost.[40]

Maintenance and preservation of the natural environment throughout the parks system is but one of many responsibilities of York County Parks. It is also charged with care of historic properties within the parks system. At this writing, ten historic sites are safely tucked within the confines of York County Parks.

Each park is unique and enhances the life of the community. Beautiful environments, absent people, in an expanding urban area would be of little note. Civic responsibility, witnessed in voluntary community service, is declining throughout the United States, but the York County Parks Department continues to benefit yearly from growing numbers of volunteers.

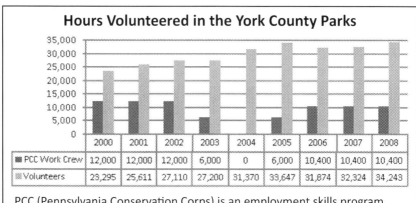

	2000	2001	2002	2003	2004	2005	2006	2007	2008
PCC Work Crew	12,000	12,000	12,000	6,000	0	6,000	10,400	10,400	10,400
Volunteers	23,295	25,611	27,110	27,200	31,370	33,647	31,874	32,324	34,243

PCC (Pennsylvania Conservation Corps) is an employment skills program for young adults sponsored by the state

According to Independent Sector, a national nonpartisan coalition of not-for-profit organizations, the dollar value of volunteer time in 2008 was estimated to be the equivalent of $20.25 per hour.[41] The number of recorded volunteer hours given to the York County Parks in 2008 was 44,643.[42] Based on the Independent Sector formula, the value of volunteer labor received by the York County Parks is equal to a contribution of $904,021. Of the $2.1 million 2008 park budget, $1,040,945 was allocated for labor, representing 49.6 percent of the budget. Uncompensated contributions by volunteers add twice as much to the allocated personnel expense. Volunteer labor is the annual equivalent of twenty-one full-time staff positions. An enormous decline in park services, maintenance, and programs would occur without this stalwart support. It is worthy of note that countless hours of volunteer service go unreported, as do many gifts in-kind.

Without volunteer support, the small paid York County Parks staff of twenty-seven could never make up the manpower hours required to operate the vast system at its current level. Broad public support earns York County Parks the reputation as one of the finest county park systems in the nation.

Seizing every opportunity to enlist volunteers, the entire staff is unfailing in reaching into the community for support, and their contagious zeal nets help. Public endorsements, community pride, and well-deserved praise are obvious examples of the department's success. Far too numerous to enumerate, a few examples of varied volunteer contributions elucidate the scope of their involvement.

Volunteer participation in the parks exploded in the fourth decade, but it began much earlier. An impressive early example of volunteer work is one of the trails at Rocky Ridge County Park, Sue's Trail. It was established to honor a young avid runner, Sue Gingrich. In December 1984, Sue was struck and killed by a car as she ran along Mt. Zion Road. Her friends and fellow members of the York Road Runners Club commemorated her life by donating countless hours to lay a two-mile trail in her honor. Spearheaded by Hal Darr, their purpose was to provide a safe alternative to running along public roads. Sue's Trail has been safely enjoyed and appreciated by thousands over the years.

From the beginning days of county parks, Boy Scouts have made generous contributions blazing trails, landscaping, and working on an endless variety of projects throughout the forty-two hundred acres of parkland.

There are jobs for every age and interest. Nonagenarians Elizabeth Winebrenner and Carl Morton offered their talents—Winebrenner as archivist, faithfully scrapbooking press accounts of park activities; Morton as the volunteer beekeeper at Nixon Park.

Starbucks employees sponsor annual walks for the parks and donate the proceeds to the parks. Their corporate headquarters doubles the walk earnings. Other team efforts by Starbucks employees include a playground at William H. Kain County Park, which they funded and installed.

A high school junior, Stacy Sisk, served at Nixon County Park Environmental Education Center two hours a week as part of an eight-week mentoring program.

Board members Ed Bievenour and Skip Durgin trained Parks Ambassadors as public relations representatives for the department. The Parks Ambassadors, established in July 2003, are hikers, bikers, equestrians, and other outdoor enthusiasts who enjoy the parks. Their mission is to influence and teach park users how to understand and care for the natural treasures within each park.

The United Way devotes a Day of Caring annually to the parks, bringing old hands and introducing new ones to park projects. Many Days of Caring result in years of caring as new volunteers emerge from the ranks of those introduced to parks at the United Way Day of Caring.

For years, Charlie Jacoby arrived, unsolicited, and planted colorful arrays of flowering annuals at John Rudy County Park and at the entry to Rocky Ridge County Park.

Dennis Mummert and Friends of the York County Astronomical Society Observatory located at John Rudy County Park sponsor annual events for the public. The observatory is a unique part of John Rudy County Park. Members of the Astronomy Club lease ground for the observatory from the parks and offer education programs for the public.

A local veterinarian and former board member, Don Patton, supported the latest park segment—Canine Meadows, a 13.5-acre enclosed off-leash dog park at John Rudy County Park. In October 2008, he sponsored the opening of Canine Meadows. A turnout of an estimated 140 excited canines, their devoted owners in tow, made the day a howling success. A Friends of Canine Meadows group was formed to oversee the area and guide activities. Bonnie Stine serves as chair of this group.

The number of worthwhile volunteer contributions to recreation activities is endless, but not the exclusive domain of park success.

Another feather in the parks' cap is land acquisition. Joe Raab's and Jack Dunn's goals have been met, and York's reputation as a place where the quality of life is high and the living is good is secure. Cost of acquisition by York County Parks has been impressive. Four of the eleven parks were acquired with a combination of county, state, and federal funds; one by lease agreement with a public utility; and five as gifts or, in one case, for the consideration of one dollar.

Efforts are underway to give added protection to parkland by implementing conservation easements, which will prevent encroachment on parkland by development or other alterations of use.

Ensuring the future of York County Parks is the sole mission of a volunteer group formed in 1986, which led to the York County Parks Foundation Charitable Trust. The trust has been ably chaired since 1991 by Dr. Luther Sowers, a retired superintendent of schools. The volunteer board is dedicated to raising and managing funds to expand parklands and facilities. Prior to the establishment of the trust, money earmarked for county parks was deposited in the general fund. The general fund employs the "squeaky wheel gets the oil" approach, so funds given to support parks might have supplemented the prison if prison needs were greater. Since the inception of the parks trust fund, there is now a secure, direct path to the parks department.

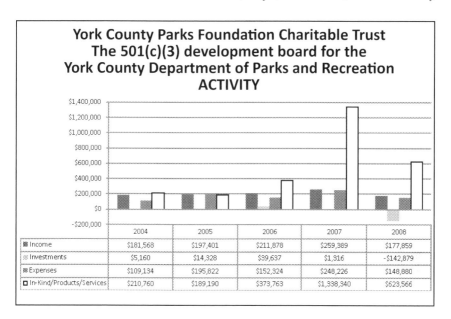

York County Parks Foundation Charitable Trust
The 501(c)(3) development board for the
York County Department of Parks and Recreation
ACTIVITY

	2004	2005	2006	2007	2008
Income	$181,568	$197,401	$211,878	$259,389	$177,859
Investments	$5,160	$14,328	$39,637	$1,316	-$142,879
Expenses	$109,134	$195,822	$152,324	$248,226	$148,880
In-Kind/Products/Services	$210,760	$189,190	$373,763	$1,338,340	$623,566

At the suggestion of William Morris, president of the York Water Company, the York County Parks Foundation Charitable Trust inaugurated the Gathering Leaves Society in 2002 to encourage planned giving and cash contributions to the parks trust. The membership ranks of the society have nearly doubled each year since its inception. Financial support for parks is also derived from small park membership fees, which have funded a fishing dock at William H. Kain County Park for people with disabilities and served to improve the wetland area at Rocky Ridge County Park.

In 1999, the first of what would become several Friends groups was formed. Members of the Friends of Wallace-Cross Mill were recruited by members of the restoration committee from five nearby churches. The Friends of Wallace-Cross Mill have identified their mission: dedication to the acquisition, preservation, and protection of the mill, through partnerships, the acquisition of artifacts, histories, structural maintenance, interpretative exhibitions of agricultural significance, and by extending educational awareness of the mill to all individuals. The Friends serve as docents and grow their ranks each year by conducting training sessions for new volunteers. They lead fundraising events and host tours on a regular basis, as well as by request throughout the year. Judy Grove, a retired teacher, serves as chair of the active group. A York County Parks staff member is delegated to provide support and guidance for the group.

In 2000, the Heritage Rail Trail County Park was designated a Millennium Trail by the White House Millennium Council. In 2001, a second volunteer group, the Friends of the Heritage Rail Trail Corridor, was established with the stated purposes of assisting York County Parks with historic preservation and interpretation of the trail and historic sites along the trail, and serving as docents for the New Freedom and Hanover Junction train stations. Peg Schlichtegry , a retired schoolteacher, serves as chair of this active group.

Former members of the Parks Board united in 2000 to organize a support group for any and all park projects, dubbing themselves the Emeritus Board. They gather throughout the year to share experiences in the parks and seek opportunities to serve park aims within and beyond park boundaries.

Nixon County Park enjoys the support of volunteers who provide ongoing assistance for the staff to extend learning opportunities at the environmental education center.

Park rangers are assisted by Park Ambassadors, a volunteer group organized in 2003. Not only are they good-will ambassadors in all the parks, they also serve as additional eyes and ears for the rangers, alerting them to violations of rules or problems they witness.

The staff seeks little recognition and deserves a lot. Longtime staffer Jeri Jones was recognized in 2006 by the National Association of Geoscience Teachers for bringing geoscience education to the general public, one of many program services Jones provides.

In 2007, Apollo Park was expanded by 191 acres owing to the generosity of the Conservation Fund. The Conservation Fund provided private funding equal to $900,000 for the expansion. The monies were supplemented by $100,000 from the York County Parks Foundation Charitable Trust.

The Natural Resource Unit of York County Parks set a ten-year wildlife forest management plan in 2001, among other things, to conduct bat counts, survey butterflies, and monitor bluebird and wood duck nest boxes. One of the most unusual services of the Natural Resource Unit is, perhaps, monitoring goose nests at Kain County Park. Eggs of the ever-growing flock of Canada geese, which have become nonmigratory, are dutifully counted each month to control the population. Before the introduction of the goose egg count, the flock numbered over six hundred. The geese first appeared in York County on their annual flight south. When they discovered few predators, lots to eat, mild winters, and a terrific lake home, they moved in and decided to stay. Aware of good York County living, they—as many of their human counterparts—became nonmigratory. It was not long until farmers near Kain County Park were frustrated by crop damage caused by the eager eaters. There was also the added public health concern posed by the risk of avian diseases. This generated an even more vital concern for a concerted effort to control the population.

The age-old adage of not counting your eggs before they hatch was not true in the case of the goose population at Kain Park. Goose eggs are meticulously inventoried and recorded by staff. When the number of eggs exceeds manageable goose population limits, the eggs are selectively eliminated. In addition to egg culling, twelve goose hunting licenses are issued annually to county residents to participate in a small, well-regulated preseason goose hunt at Kain Park. It is the only other legally sanctioned means of goose population control the department has in place. On the appointed day, hunters have discovered that at the first blush of dawn they have, at most, one chance to target their goose. As sound from the first gun breaks the morning silence, signaling the beginning of the hunting day, it ends. Not officially, but because when the canny geese hear gunfire, they immediately take flight to seek safe haven beyond the range of the guns and outside the boundaries of the park. None return until dusk. It is basically a one-chance-only hunt.

Other work by the Natural Resource Unit centers around shoreline stabilization at the lakes; stream restoration in Spring Valley County Park; and stocking trout in the Codorus Creek, which flows through Spring Valley County Park and Kain County Park. These projects are done in cooperation with the Pennsylvania Conservation Corps, the Izaak Walton League, and the Pennsylvania Fish and Boat Commission.

In 2008 the parks building and grounds team maintained 4,200 acres of parkland plus a physical inventory of 57 picnic pavilions and shelters, 30 restrooms, 10 historic sites, 140 acres of grass athletic fields, 400 picnic tables, 1,600 parking spaces, 34 parking lots, and 22 sport fields and playgrounds.

Sandwiched between duties is ongoing staff training: CPR certifications, pesticide application permits, CDL licensing for Penn DOT, training in electrical work, fire training, computer skills, and a myriad of other training requirements essential to managing a large system effectively. Ironically, the staff has received instruction for nuclear emergencies. The department maintains a supply of radiation medication for use in the event of a nuclear event at Three Mile Island or Peach Bottom Electric. Each nuclear power plant is in near proximity to a county park.

Volunteers also extend hospitality. In April 2008, Sandy Cooley, a former board chairman and staunch champion of parks, chaired a memorable evening to celebrate the fortieth anniversary of the York County Parks. Several hundred parks devotees shared dinner and memories. The room filled with volunteers did not fail to capitalize on the evening. Event sponsors, a printed program with congratulatory advertisements, and a silent auction raised $25,000 for York County Parks by evening's end.

The enduring quest of human nature for order and stability is often intensified by the constancy of change. Recognition of the unalterable change posed by loss of an irreplaceable site in York County resulted in the formation of a consortium of government groups and agencies, part of a regional initiative to encourage cultural tourism. Their aim was to preserve scenic and historic land along the Susquehanna River.

A group of like-minded advocates, including representatives from the Lancaster York Heritage Region, the Pennsylvania Department of Conservation and Natural Resources, the Farm and Natural Lands Trust of York County, Lower Windsor Township, and the York County Board of Commissioners, was concerned about a certain parcel threatened by development. The site has significance culturally, scientifically, socially, archaeologically, environmentally, and historically. It is a pristine, largely undeveloped, parcel of nearly nine hundred acres abutting the Susquehanna River. It is situated on, arguably, one of most magnificent river overlooks to be found on the planet. It was, in fact, one of a few sites winnowed from many in the eighteenth century considered as a place for the capital city of the new republic. In the end, it was a close runner-up to the site along the Potomac River that was ultimately selected as the nation's capital. Eons earlier, the beauty of the Susquehanna overlook had not gone unnoticed by the Susquehannock Indians, for whom it served as a cherished gathering spot for centuries.

The group sought to acquire some, if not all, of the land. Their efforts resulted in a chain of events that embroiled York County in a bitter legal dispute. By the time the dust settled, acquisition of a seventy-nine-acre parcel now known as Highpoint Scenic Vista and Recreation Area, and 187 acres now known as Native Lands County Park, was extracted from 266 acres of the original nine hundred acre parcel.

York County Parks was aware of the river site and had, in fact, been approached in 1991 by a group seeking to preserve the property.[43] The board endorsed efforts of the group, but lacking funds, the acquisition efforts failed to materialize at that time. Years later, when the issue resurfaced, the York County Parks Board was not included.

County of York Chief Clerk Chuck Noll reported the cost of the legal dispute for the two parcels totaled $45 million. The owner of a $150,000 house in York County will pay an added seventeen dollars annually for five years in accordance with the court-ordered settlement. After five years, the amount due will be reduced to an annual sum of eleven dollars for twenty-five years.

Following acquisition, a newly elected York County Board of Commissioners vested custody of Highpoint Scenic Vista and Native Lands into the hands of York County Parks. The effort waged had centered on a debate involving government land acquisition, and the protracted legal battle polarized the community. A reminder of the admonition of Maurice Goddard in 1955.

> *"Acquiring parks and open spaces for parks in and around urban centers must be regarded as a 'now or never' proposition ... such a program simply cannot be postponed until sometime in the remote and hazy future, because land costs in these areas, high as they are now, will be too high for government purchase in another ten years."*
>
> *Honorable Maurice Goddard, 1955*
> *Pennsylvania Secretary, Department of Environmental*
> *Resources, and the Susquehanna River Basin Commission*

Although the board of the York County Parks Department had no involvement in the efforts initiated to secure these parcels, the decision to put the controversial property into the hands of York County Parks was a wise one. York County Parks has frugally managed every penny of its spartan budget for forty years, providing land and recreation at an incredible bargain. The 421,049 residents of York County paid $1.34 per person in taxes per park visit in 2008.

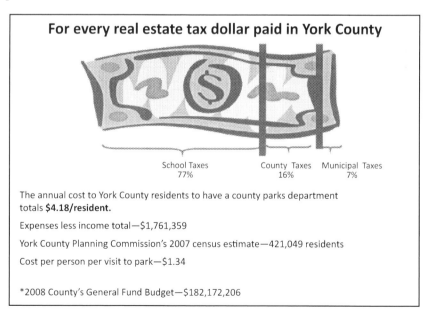

For every real estate tax dollar paid in York County

| School Taxes | County Taxes | Municipal Taxes |
| 77% | 16% | 7% |

The annual cost to York County residents to have a county parks department totals **$4.18/resident.**

Expenses less income total—$1,761,359

York County Planning Commission's 2007 census estimate—421,049 residents

Cost per person per visit to park—$1.34

*2008 County's General Fund Budget—$182,172,206

The popular parks and historic sites within park bounds attracted 1,312,249 visitors in 2008. The number of users rises annually. Measured by resident, the cost for York County Parks before the addition of Highpoint and Native Lands was $4.18 per person—a stellar accomplishment. Much of the success of the York County Parks can be attributed to financial prudence, public support, and transparency.

York County Parks leadership is legendary. Awards line the walls hailing the director, staff, and volunteers for countless leadership contributions. Many are tucked away.[44] The board and army of volunteers of the county parks find and thrust talented citizens into leadership roles, always seeking consensus. Park task forces are led by respected leaders who embody the ideals of public service and have a basic understanding of the essential need for transparency to gain public support for projects. York County Parks is one of the most visible, popular arms of government, with a reputation for cautious decision making.

Up until the end of the 1990s, the fifty-four departments of York County government reported individually to the York County Commissioners. This unwieldy system was revised at the direction of the commissioners by the newly appointed chief clerk, Chuck Noll. Noll reframed the outmoded system to streamline communication and accountability of the various departments. Employing the private sector paradigm of *best practices,* Noll identified six basic categories within the fifty-four departments. Six executive directors were appointed by the commissioners from the ranks of the fifty-four departments and given administrative oversight of the new organizational structure. Each department now operates under one of six management categories with similar missions. The reorganization has proven to be a cost-effective change and resulted in efficiency in resource allocation and personnel. The six broad areas encapsulating the fifty-four York County departments are:

> Information Technology
> Human Services
> Emergency Services
> Human Resources
> Facility Management
> Parks and Natural Resources

Reflecting on the consideration of the six criteria for the evaluation of public policy put forth in the opening pages of this account will put the worth of the York County Department of Parks and Recreation in perspective.

1. A public need must be recognized.

York County Parks transparently seeks and meets public needs for parkland now and in the future.

2. A plan to meet the need must be developed.

The York County Parks' realistic park planning and acquisition is exemplary, working in concert with the York County Planning Department so county needs are identified and addressed.

3. A source of funding must be available.

York County Parks pursues and expends funding from public and private sources using well-defined goals within its budgetary guidelines, which are almost always limited.

4. A dynamic leader must advocate the benefits.

There are no better advocates for the York County Parks than the highly-professional staff and the wide-ranging volunteer citizen supporters. Department communications are frequent, clear, responsive, and far-reaching.

5. A positive public response must be elicited.

Public response to the York County Parks extends beyond the boundaries of the county and has brought national acclaim to the department.

6. An administrative or legislative mandate must vest authority for implementation of the policy in accountable, competent, dedicated hands in a timely way.

The York County Commissioners have entrusted the executive director, board, and staff of the department with responsibility for the present and future of county parkland, and the department has demonstrated accountability for the trust vested in it, earning public support and respect throughout its history.

Not a department to rest on its laurels, the near future of York County Parks is filled with innovative approaches to efficient maintenance of parkland in the face of an epic economic crisis. Practical efforts demonstrate its effectiveness. A major tree harvest at Rocky Ridge County Park will eliminate insect damage to trees and provide lumber for park use as well as income. A popular picnic pavilion area has added a year-round restroom facility to increase rental availability and income.

The pursuit of additional land adjacent to Apollo Park, presently owned by public utility companies, continues. A 2008 Operation Planning Review facilitated by the Center for Community Engagement at York College is in progress.

Rudy County Park is the home of the York County Envirothon competition. Phase II of the northern extension of the York County Heritage Rail Trail from Crist Field to U.S. Route 30 continues in cooperation with the Rail Trail Authority. The park rules and regulations are routinely reviewed and updated. The staff collaborates with volunteers to foster new and ongoing relationships. Ever the frugal budget guardians, York County Parks stretches every penny at its disposal, demonstrating amazing results of making much of very little.

In 2009 Tom Brant retired with an exemplary record of service as Director. In 2010 the York County Commissioners named Tammy Klunk to the position. Klunk holds a B.A. from York College of Pennsylvania in Recreation and Leisure Studies. She joined the ranks of the Parks Department upon graduation and has paid her dues in numerous roles for the Department. Her work has been extraordinary and the citizens of York County can be pleased with her efforts on their behalf. There is little doubt Klunk will continue to distinguish herself as she steps into her new role as Director of the York County Parks Department.

The well-defined goals of York County Parks call for prudence in every nook and cranny of the system to sustain the level of excellence for which it is noted. It is a tough assignment in tough times, but there is no doubt the York County Department of Parks and Recreation is earnest in its mission and vigilant in bringing much to many, for very little.

> *"The ultimate test of a moral society is the kind of world that it leaves to its children."*
>
> *Dietrich Bonhoeffer, German theologian*
> *(1906–1945)*

View of Susquehanna River from the summit of Highpoint County Park

Hikers at Apollo County Park

Visitors outside Richard Nixon Nature Center

Members of The Gathering Leaves Society at Richard Nixon Nature Center

The Wallace Cross Mill following restoration

Archaeological dig at P. Joseph Raab Count Park

Little Brown Pipestrelle Bat clinging to his mine shaft home at P. Joseph Raab County Park

The bow of a kayak on Lake Williams at William H. Kain County Park.

Keegan Fobes casting a line into Lake Redman at the William H. Kain County Park

Time for reflection along the banks of Lake Williams.

Gold panning at Spring Valley County Park

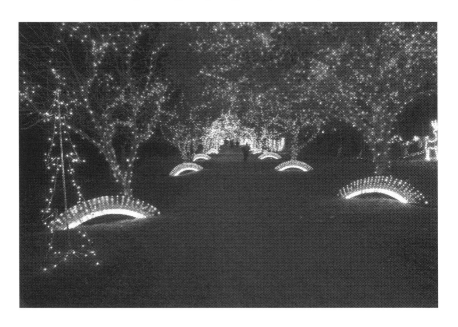

Christmas Magic along the Rainbow Trail at Rocky Ridge County Park.

Former migratory geese enjoying their idea of the best place in York
County for geese, The William H. Kain County Park.

The York County Parks maintenance crew.(year) left to right
Douglas Stough, Todd Hampson, Tim Shealer, Kerry Flinchbaugh,
Grant Bolton, Jerry Broome, Joshua DeWees, Terry Grothe, Randy
Leiphart, Thomas Hansberry, Peter Rodriques, Douglas Murphy.
On tractor is Roger Brunner

Frolicking dogs at Canine Meadows in John Rudy County Park

Howard Tunnel, one of the landmarks along
the Heritage Rail Trail County Park

Appendix A

York County Department of Parks and Recreation Statements

Mission Statement

York County Department of Parks and Recreation enhances the quality of community life acting as a steward for the environment. In this capacity, it acquires, conserves, and manages park lands and offers a variety of recreational and educational opportunities.

Value Statement

As steward of the county's park lands, York County Department of Parks and Recreation:

- Creates customer-friendly environments.
- Provides a diversity of natural areas to promote passive recreation.
- Conserves and interprets the natural and historical aspects of park resources.
- Emphasizes preservation and creation of wildlife and plant habitat.
- Listens and responds to park users.
- Encourages safe and responsible use of park resources.
- Maintains the highest level of professionalism.
- Enters into partnerships and pursues networking.
- Promotes and honors volunteer participation.

- Fosters innovation and creativity in fulfilling mission responsibilities.
- Cultivates new sources of support and funding.

Vision Statement

York County Department of Parks and Recreation strives to be the county leader in environmental conservation, preservation, and education. Programs and projects in these areas reflect sound management and stewardship principles and a strong organizational commitment to innovation and public service.

Appendix B

About the Parks ...

Rocky Ridge County Park (1968 – 750 acres)

The first park is perched on a mature, oak-covered hillside off Deininger Road northwest of Hellam. Features include: three traditional day-use recreation/picnic areas, eleven pavilions, twelve miles of multiuse (hike-horse-bike) trails, observation decks, softball field, volleyball court, playgrounds, fitness trail, and home of Christmas Magic—A Festival of Lights.

Directions: From U.S. Route 30, take Mt. Zion Road (PA Route 24) north for 1 mile; turn right onto Deininger Road and follow into park.

Richard M. Nixon County Park (1968 – 171 acres)

Established through a gift of land from Bob Hoffman, founder of York Barbell, as the county's second park and named after the newly elected U.S. president. Includes a fourteen thousand-square foot Nature Center with a focus on environmental education, including a museum with 170 wildlife mounts set in associated dioramas. Also has six miles of hiking trails, with a wide variety of plants and animal life, with a small stream. This park adjoins Kain County Park and the Hollow Creek Greenway.

Directions: From York, follow South George Street through Jacobus to Valley Road; turn right; follow road .8 mile to bottom of hill; turn right onto Nixon Drive; go one block; turn left and follow to park.

Apollo County Park (1969 – 340 acres)

Established through a gift of land by P. H. Glatfleter Co., Inc., and named in honor of the 1969 Apollo moon landing. The park borders the Susquehanna River with hills, valleys, and streams, featuring mountain laurel, hemlock, and tulip poplar trees. Three miles of trails and the Mason-Dixon Trail traverse this park.

Directions: Take PA Route 74 south to Burkholder Road; turn left to Boyd Road, and parking lot is at the end of the road—or continue on Burkholder Road; turn left on Shenks Ferry Road, and parking lot is on the left.

Spring Valley County Park (1972 – 868 acres)

Located on the headwaters of the East Branch of Codorus Creek and Lake Redman and named after the "Valleys of Springs." The East Branch, a stocked trout stream, rolls through old farm fields in the park and is the center of five miles of multiuse trails, a fish-for-fun pond, a dog training area, an animal activity area, and two pavilions.

Directions: From I-83 take Glen Rock exit; travel east on PA Route 216 for .1 mile; turn right onto Potosi Road and travel 2.1 miles to Crest Road, where the park begins. The animal activity area is on Crest Road; fishing areas and Fish-for-Fun are located on Lehr Road.

John C. Rudy County Park (1973 – 150 acres)

Donated by the John and Viola Rudy family, and home of the Parks Department's administrative headquarters, located in the 1798 farmhouse. The headquarters is listed on the National Registry of Historic Places as an historic farmstead and adjoins the Codorus Creek. Park facilities include: picnic pavilions, flush restrooms, soccer and softball fields, volleyball courts, horseshoe pits, large playgrounds, open fields and space, a 5K cross-country course, BMX track, observatory, sundial garden, gardens by Penn State Master Gardeners, a 1.2-mile paved loop trail open to biking, hiking, jogging, and Rollerblading, and the northern trailhead of the Heritage Rail Trail County Park. Home of Canine Meadows, a 13.5-acre, off-leash dog area supported by the Friends of Canine Meadows and also the site of the York County Parks Hot Air Balloon Festival.

Directions: From U.S. Route 30, follow Sherman Street north 2.2 miles to traffic light; turn right; go .1 mile, turn left at traffic light continuing along North Sherman Street; go .5 mile; turn left to Mundis Race Road, and park is .5 mile on right.

William H. Kain County Park (1976 – 1,637 acres)

Lake Redman (290 acres) and Lake Williams (220 acres) are the main attractions of this park. The York Water Company leases these lands to York County for public recreation, representing the first public-private partnership in the nation. Fishing, boating, pavilions, twelve miles of multiuse trails, horseshoe pits, volleyball, remote-controlled airplane and boat areas, annual concerts, and a playground are available. The park operates a boat concession and offers nonmotorized boats for rent. This park adjoins Nixon County Park and the Hollow Creek Greenway.

Directions: From York, follow South George Street to Jacobus. For Lake Redman, turn left onto Church Street and go .6 mile to boat launch area on left. For Lake Williams, turn right onto Water Street and go .5 mile to main parking area.

Heritage Rail Trail County Park (1990 – 176 acres)

Stretching from York City south to the Maryland state line below New Freedom and connecting to Maryland's NCR trail for another twenty miles, this linear park was once the Northern Central Railroad and was acquired from the Commonwealth of Pennsylvania for one dollar. Extending more than twenty-one miles through eleven different municipalities, the trail is a ten-foot-wide path of compacted stone designed for hiking, bicycling, running, nature watching, and horseback riding. The rails are still active per the Pennsylvania Public Utility Commission. This park offers seven sites listed on the National Registry of Historic Places. Friends of the Heritage Rail Corridor support the museums at Hanover Junction and New Freedom Train Stations.

Directions: Parking lots are conveniently located in New Freedom, Railroad, Glen Rock, Hanover Junction, Seven Valleys, Glatfelter Station, Brillhart Station, and downtown York.

P. Joseph Raab County Park (1993 – 73 acres)

Acquired through a land donation by Modern Landfill and located between Jefferson and Seven Valleys. The park is listed on the National Registry of Historic Places. The York Iron Company mine occupied the property and was one of the finest ore-producing mines between 1850 and 1880. Features include the bat caves, as a result of the mining industry, three miles of trails, and a small stream. Named in honor of the "father" of the park system, P. Joseph Raab.

Directions: From U.S. Route 30, turn onto PA Route 616 south; turn right on Green Valley Road; right on Hoff Road, and follow to parking lot located on the left.

Wallace-Cross Mill Historic Site (1997) slightly over one acre

Provided as a donation to York County by Harry Cross in 1978, with the initial mill restoration completed in 1999. The mill is an 1826 three-story wooden building that is a water-powered custom operating grist mill listed on the National Registry of Historic Places and supported by the Friends of Wallace-Cross Mill.

Directions: From Stewartstown, take Main Street (Rt. 24) north out of Stewartstown; turn right on Hickory Road; then left onto Cross Mill Road; follow until you see mill on right.

Highpoint Scenic Vista and Recreation Area (2007 – 79 acres)

This park offers a spectacular 360-degree view of the Susquehanna River, meadowlands, and surrounding hills and counties. The main ADA walking path leading to the summit rises 110 vertical feet over its half-mile route, with additional grass trails. The Mason-Dixon Trail traverses this park.

Directions: From U.S. Route 30, take the Wrightsville Exit; turn south and proceed .7 mile on Cool Springs Road to traffic light; continue straight through traffic light; travel .9 miles, then turn left on Knights View Road; turn left on Hilt Road, and ADA parking lot is on right.

Native Lands County Park (2009 – 187 acres)

This park features hiking, with many views of the Susquehanna River, bird-watching, nature observation, and a historic site of the Susquehanna Indians. A six-foot-wide mowed trail, approximately 1.5 miles in length, traverses the property in a north/south direction.

Directions: From U.S. Route 30, take Wrightsville exit. Turn south on Cool Springs Road to traffic light for .7 miles. Proceed (south) straight through traffic light for 1.7 miles. Turn left on Knights View Road for 1.5 miles, then right on PA Route 624 south. Travel 1.5 miles and turn right into Kline's Run Park. Park in grass near portable toilets, and look for signs to Native Lands Heritage Trail.

Appendix C

Charts

Available Park Facilities

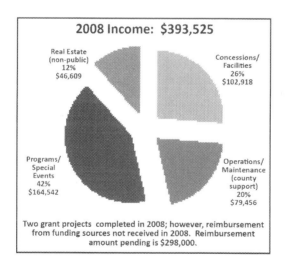

2008 Income: $393,525

Real Estate (non-public)
12%
$46,609

Concessions/ Facilities
26%
$102,918

Programs/ Special Events
42%
$164,542

Operations/ Maintenance (county support)
20%
$79,456

Two grant projects completed in 2008; however, reimbursement from funding sources not received in 2008. Reimbursement amount pending is $298,000.

Budget Pie Chart

Appendix D

York County Board of Commissioners

1964–1967	H C. Busser, Horace M. Grove, Carl L. Hykes
1968–1971	P. Joseph Raab, Allen C. Spangler, Charles A. Stein Jr.
1972–1975	Charles A. Stein Jr., William McKinley, Caroll H. Leppo
1976–1979	Robert L. Bowers, William McKinley, Caroll H. Leppo
1980–1983	Robert L. Bowers, William McKinley, Jay R. Bair
1984–1987	Lorraine B. Hovis, William McKinley, Jay R. Bair
1988–1991	Lorraine B. Hovis, George M. Trout, Ronald E. Fitzkee
1992–1995	George M. Trout, Robert A. Minnich, Newton D. Brown
1996–1999	Robert A. Minnich, Christopher B. Reilly, Shirley L. Glass
2000–2003	Robert A. Minnich, Christopher B. Reilly, Shirley L. Glass
	Minnich died in 2000; James F. Donahue completed term
2004–2007	Lori O. Mitrick, Douglas Kilgore, Steven M. Chronister
2008–2011	Steven M. Chronister, Christopher B. Reilly, Doug Hoke

Appendix E

Park Directors

1968–1970	William Erhman (part-time)
1970–1976	William Erhman (full-time)
1976–1977	Duane Close
1977–1978	Tom Krebs (interim)
1978–1979	Paul Wojciechowski
1980	Tom Krebs
1980–1994	Guy Walker
1994–2009	Tom Brant
2010	Tammy Klunk

APPENDIX F

York County Advisory Board of Parks & Recreation Chairs

1968–1970	Harry J. McLaughlin
1971–1988	Reverend Carroll C. Luckenbaugh
1989–1990	Thomas Clough
1991–1994	Charles H. Falkler
1995–1998	Sandra E. Cooley
1999–2005	Duane R. Close
2006–present	Sean "Skip" Durgin

Appendix G

York County Parks Advisory Board

Sean "Skip" Durgin, Chairman
John Strine, Vice Chairman
Deirdre Folkers, Secretary
Thomas Englerth
Jan Klinedinst
Steve Lentz
John Rinehart
Nancy Seiling
Anne Walko

    This volunteer board serves as a liaison between the parks and the public. The public is encouraged to attend board meetings, held the fourth Tuesday of each month, at 7:00 p.m. at Pleasant Acres.

APPENDIX H

York County Parks Foundation Charitable Trust

Luther B. Sowers, Chairman
George "Skip" Lehmann, Vice Chairman
Linda B. Davidson, Secretary
William T. Morris, Treasurer
Thomas R. Brant
Betsy B. Lehner
Milton J. Menchey
Don Patton
Steven Ricklefs
Dale L. Schaeberle
Timothy E. Senft

This volunteer board is dedicated to raising and managing funds to expand park lands and facilities.

Appendix I

Past Advisory Board Members and Emeritus Board Members

(*denotes Emeritus Board Member)

J. Kerr Anderson*
John (Jack) F. Barbor*
Jack Barnhart
Edward L. Bievenour*
James Brett
Duane R. Close*
Thomas F. Clough*
C. Harold Conrad
Sandra E. Cooley*
J. Richard Cooper*
Rev. Harold Crouse
J. Elmer Crowl
G. M. David
Felicia Dell
Rebecca Dittenhafer
Reed "Jack" Dunn Jr. *
Joseph Edwards
Charles H. Falkler
Voni Grimes*
Larry C. Heim
Donald G. Heisler*
Carroll F. Hunt

J. Robert Katherman, Esq.*
Jeff Kuhn
George "Skip" Lehmann*
Rev. Carroll C. Luckenbaugh*
Frank McKee
Harry J. McLaughlin
Sylvia Newcombe
Don Patton*
Joseph K. Pierce
P. Joseph Raab
James L. Rebert
John Rinehart*
Glenn L. Rohrbaugh
Tim Senft
Robert Seybold
Eleanor Boggs Shoemaker*
Phillip Stinger
Mike Summers
Grant Voaden
Anne K. Wagner*
Roy J. Wagner Jr.
Julie Weaver
Ray R. Wiegand
David Wildasin
John Wurzbacher

Appendix J

York County Rail Trail Authority
Members, Present and Past

Present

Carl Knoch
Don Gogniat
Ed Hughes
Glenn R. Eyster Jr.
Henry Herrman
Pamela Gay
Dwight R. Robison Jr.
Heidi Hormel
Mack Johnson
Jonathan Pinkerton

Past

Tom Austin
Scott Beaverson, Esq.
Jon Bergdoll
Oscar E. Fox
Tim Fulton
Sara Hunt
Bill Knepper
John O'Keefe

Jeff Osman
Margaret Prevot
Charles Rupp
Rev. J. Thomas Shelley
Thomas Warman
Stephen R. Winand

APPENDIX K

Gathering Leaves Society

The York County Parks Foundation Charitable Trust announced the creation of the "Gathering Leaves Society" in October 2002. The Society honors those who have provided for the stewardship of the York County Parks over the long term, either through a planned gift or cash donation to the endowment fund. Members as of 2008 include:

J. Kerr Anderson
John F. Barbor
Mary & Cooper Boyd
Tom & RuthAnn Brant
Eileen & Duane Close
Donald C. Dallmeyer
Dave & Linda Davidson
Burnell Diehl
James F. Donahue
Ronald L. & Sharon A. Dorn
Roberta A. Downs
Shawn & Skip Durgin
John L. Finlayson
Ronald Foulis
Michael P. Gavin
Robert Glass
Arthur J. Glatfelter
Judith Grove
L. C. Heim
Don & Donallene Heisler

Carroll & Irene Hunt
Nancy F. Keiser
Paul H. Keiser
L. Jeani Kiser
Sue Ann Kline
Truman & Darlene Kling
Maxine & William Klunk
Tammy F. Klunk
Raymond E. Knowles Jr.
Ann & George Lehmann
Betsy Lehner
Larry S. Lehner
Donna Meanner
Sandy & Bud Menchey
Nancy S. Morris
William T. Morris
Mr. & Mrs. Irvin S. Naylor
R. Scott Neely
Paul E. Newcomer
Tom & Joan Norris
Don & Dee Patton
Chris & Lisa Reilly
Fred D. & Mary E. Reiss
Steve & Elizabeth Ricklefs
John M. & Rebecca Rinehart
Dale L. Schaeberle
Timothy Senft
Roger E. Shaffer
Eleanor Boggs Shoemaker
Jim & Nancy Rae Sieling
Ruth & Luther Sowers
John & Lisa Strine
Paul & Kathryn Summers
John & Joan Ulrich

In Remembrance of Members:

Shirley Glass
Geneva Bowman Kaltreider
Sydney Levitan
Ruth M. Sponsler

If you have provided for the York County Parks through your estate or a planned gift, and are not listed, or if you want information on how to become a member, please contact us.

York County Parks Foundation Charitable Trust
400 Mundis Race Road
York, PA 17406
717.840.7227

Appendix L

Members of Friends Organizations

Current Friends of Wallace-Cross Mill

Judy Grove, Chair
Larry Collins
Ann Davis
Todd Eyster
Betty Lou Green
Karen Marsteller
Connie Searle
Eleanor Boggs Shoemaker
H. Vernon Tyson
Steve Uzmed

Current Friends of the Heritage Rail Trail

Peggy Schlichter, Chair
Linda Bugash
Ray Kinard
Kathy Kotzman
Chuck Neal
Dennis Norton
Gerald Reese
Susan Rizer
Allen Smith
Chris Snyder

Mikele Stillman
Shirley Strayer

Current Friends of Canine Meadows

Bonnie Stine, Chair
Deana Albright
Michelle Busch-Young
Monique Lambert
Barb Markel
Ann Mummert
Barbara & Ross Raffensperger
Carol Stephens
Elaine Weems

Appendix M

Current Staff, York County Department of Parks & Recreation

1983–present	Tammy F. Klunk, Assistant Director
1995–present	Gerald R. Ford Jr., Chief Ranger, Ranger Unit
1991–present	Michael E. Fobes, Manager, Natural Resource Unit
1999–present	Barry L. Myers, Superintendent, Building & Grounds Unit
1984–present	Francis A. Velázquez, Manager, Education & Outreach Unit
2001–present	George H. Howett, Assistant Superintendent, Buildings & Grounds Unit
2004–present	Todd A. Hampson, Assistant Superintendent, Buildings & Grounds Unit
1979–present	Jeri L. Jones , Program Coordinator
2007–present	Amber L. Carothers, Naturalist II
2008–present	Patricia M. Chamberlin, Naturalist II
2000–present	Deborah A. Carbaugh, Administrative Assistant
2002–present	Kay A. Kraft, Administrative Support
1988–present	R. Scott Neely, Ranger II
1994–present	Ronald Heist, Ranger II
1999–present	James Brown, Ranger II
1995–present	Richard Rudacille, Ranger II

Current Buildings and Grounds Unit Staff:

Grant Bolton
Tom Hansberry
Randy Leiphart
Terry Grothe
Kerry Flinchbaugh
Roger Brunner
Dug Stough
Jerry Broome
Josh Dewees
Douglas Murphy
Keith Hawkins
Joe Carbaugh

APPENDIX N

York County Parks Mileposts

1968—Commissioners (President Commissioner P. Joseph Raab) established York County Board of Parks & Recreation.

1968—Rocky Ridge County Park purchased.

1968—Nixon County Park established through a land donation from Bob Hoffman in honor of newly elected U.S. president.

1969—Apollo County Park established through a donation from P. H. Glatfelter in honor of the Apollo moon landing.

1970—First park director hired.

1972—Spring Valley County Park acquired partially through eminent domain.

1973—John Rudy County Park established through a land donation in memory of John and Mary Rudy.

1976—William H. Kain County Park established through an agreement with the York Water Company (landowner).

1978—Nixon County Park Nature Center opens.

1984—First Christmas Magic program.

1986—York County Parks Charitable Trust established.

1988—U.S. President Nixon visited Nixon Park.

1990—Heritage Rail Trail County Park purchased from the Commonwealth of Pennsylvania for one dollar.

1992—Treasury of Wildlife Wing dedicated (Nixon Park Nature Center).

1993—P. Joseph Raab County Park established through a land donation from Waste Management, Inc.

1996—First park-wide Strategic Plan (second plan completed 2001).

1997—Cross Mill placed under the management of the York County Parks.

1998—Park-wide membership/newsletter *Fox Tracks* created.

1998—Park endowment formed with the York County Community Foundation.

1998—John Rudy County Park Master Site Plan completed.

1999—Friends of Wallace-Cross Mill established.

1999—Heritage Rail Trail County Park trail construction completed (into York City).

2000—Trail system designated as a Millennium Trail by the White House Millennium Council.

2000—Emeritus Board established.

2001—Friends of Heritage Rail Trail Corridor established.

2001—Hanover Junction Train Station Restoration completed and dedicated.

2001—First parking lot constructed at Apollo Park.

2002—Gathering Leaves Society established.

2003—Rocky Ridge County Park Master Site Plan completed.

2003—Park Ambassadors program established.

2003—New Freedom Train Station Restoration completed and dedicated.

2003—Howard Tunnel restored and dedicated.

2004—Maintenance complex built at Rudy Park.

2004—Inaugural Hot Air Balloon Festival.

2005—Raab County Park opened to public.

2006—Park visitation reached one million annual visitors.

2007—Northern Extension Rail Trail–Phase I. completed

2007—Apollo County Park expanded by 191 acres.

2007—Highpoint Scenic Vista & Recreation Area acquired.

2008—Friends of Canine Meadows formed.

2009—Native Lands County Park acquired.

Appendix O

National Register of Historic Places Maintained by York County Department of Parks & Recreation

#	NAME	LOCATION	LISTED
1	**Wallace-Cross Mill** (PA Inventory of Historic Places 3/2/77) *BUILT: 1826*	**15759 Cross Mill Road Felton, PA 17322 East Hopewell Township**	**12/22/77**
2	**Hanover Junction Railroad Station** *BUILT: 1852*	**2433 Seven Valleys Road Seven Valleys, PA 17360 North Codorus Township** *Rail Trail Park*	**12/29/83**
3	**York Iron Co. Mine**	**Green Valley Road & Hoff Road North Codorus Township** *Raab Park*	**03/15/85**

4	New Freedom Railroad Station *BUILT: 1865*	117 North Front Street New Freedom, PA 17349 New Freedom Borough *Rail Trail Park*	05/04/95
5	MP 38.93 Stone Arch Bridge *BUILT: 1871*	1st stone arch bridge north of New Freedom on Rt. 616 Shrewsbury Township *Rail Trail Park*	05/04/95
6	MP 40.39 Stone Arch Bridge *BUILT: 1871*	1st stone arch bridge south of Glen Rock on Rt. 616 Shrewsbury Township *Rail Trail Park*	05/04/95
7	MP 44.16 Bridge *BUILT: 1835*	Located at Larue Springfield Township *Rail Trail Park*	05/04/95
8	MP 47.00 Metal Railroad Bridge BUILT: 1900	Borough of Seven Valleys on Rt. 214 Seven Valleys Borough *Rail Trail Park*	05/04/95
9	Howard Tunnel *BUILT: 1840 & 1868*	North Codorus Township *Rail Trail Park*	05/19/95
10	Bixler Farmstead *BUILT:* *House & Summer House: 1798* *Barn: 1805*	400 Mundis Race Road York, PA 17402 East Manchester Township *Rudy Park*	07/27/00

APPENDIX P

Recent Major Awards and Special Events of York County Parks

1999

- Historic York: 1999 Preservation Award.
- York County Chamber of Commerce: Certificate of Recognition (Cross Mill being first county property restored in the name of agriculture).

2000

- NACPRO (National Association of County Park and Recreation Officials): Thomas R. Brant (named "Outstanding Public Official").
- Pennsylvania Wildlife Federation Conservation Organization: Award to York County Rail Trail Authority.
- PennDOT: Diamond Award for Engineering Excellence for work along Heritage Rail Trail County Park to York County Parks and C. S. Davidson, Inc.
- Pennsylvania Conservation Corps: attended National Association of Service and Conservation Corps service project.
- White House Millennium Council: Millennium Trail designation for parkwide trails.
- York County Conservation District: recognized Thomas R. Brant for eight years of service to district.
- Historic York: Preservation Award to Cross Mill.
- Make-A-Wish: recognized York County Parks for participation.

- Francis Velazquez presented teacher training program at National Environmental Education Conference.

2001

- Preservation PA: PA Historic Preservation Initiative Award for restoration and preservation work of ten historic structures.
- Pennsylvania Department of Labor & Industry: Secretary's Award by Johnny Bulter, Secretary of Labor & Industry, recognized continued support of the Pennsylvania Conservation Corps program by York County Parks.
- Pennsylvania Department of Transportation: Agility Program Award for participation in the Agility Program.

2002

- Pennsylvania Recreation and Parks Society Publication and Promotion Award: presented at the State PRPS conference recognizing the York County Parks 2001 Annual Report.
- 2002 Outstanding Conservation Educator: York County Conservation District presented Joy Howell, naturalist, Nixon Park, this award.
- Preservation Award: Historic York, Inc., presented this award recognizing the restoration of the Hanover Junction Train Station.
- Certificate of Appreciation: The York Water Company recognized the department "for efforts in doing our part in conserving water during the drought of 2002."
- Certificate of Appreciation: The York County Commissioners recognized the department for "participation in the Codorus Creek cleanup for a cleaner and safer community."
- First presentation of the "Park Achievement Award": This new award recognizes an individual or group of individuals for their extraordinary service and dedication to the York County Parks and will be presented annually. On March 5, 2002, at the First Annual Volunteer Recognition Reception, this award was presented to the founding members of the Parks Board: Harry J. McLaughlin, Chairman; J. Kerr Anderson; Voni B. Grimes; Carroll F. Hunt; Rev. Carroll C. Luckenbaugh; and John R. Rinehart.

2003

- 35th Anniversary Recognition

—Citation, Pennsylvania Senate
—Citation, Pennsylvania House of Representatives
—Proclamation, York County Board of Commissioners
- Rail-Trail Design Recognition Award: Presented by the Rail Trail Conservancy and the American Society of Landscape Architects recognizing the Heritage Rail Trail County Park.
- Special Customer Recognition: Presented by the Shadowfax Corporation recognizing the York County Parks as a long-term customer of their services.

2004

National Association of County Parks and Recreation Officials: "Certificate of Excellence"
—Friends of the York County Parks—Outstanding Support Organization
—York County Parks Maintenance Facility—Parks and Recreation Maintenance Facility
—Nixon Park Environmental Education—Parks and Recreation Program Award
- U.S. Department of Transportation, Federal Highway Administration: "Excellence Award"
—Howard Tunnel Rehabilitation
- Pennsylvania Recreation & Park Society: "Excellence of Programming Awards"
—Nixon County Park Environmental Education Curriculum Program Award
—New Freedom Train Station—Historic/Social/Culture Site Program Award
- Preservation Pennsylvania and Pennsylvania Historical and Museum Commission
—Howard Tunnel Restoration—2004 Pennsylvania Historic Preservation Award
- Historic York, Inc.: "Preservation Award"
—Howard Tunnel Restoration
York County Community Foundation: "Energy Program Award"
—Nixon County Park Environmental Education Center
- Northeast Regional Master Gardener: "Search for Excellence Award"
—Trials Gardens at John Rudy County Park

2005

- National Association of County Parks and Recreation officials: "Certificate of Excellence"
  —Hot Air Balloon Festival
- Pennsylvania Recreation & Park Society: "Excellence in Programming Awards
  —Hot Air Balloon Festival
  —Trailhead Improvements Partnership collaborative effort to improve the Lafayette Plaza information kiosk
- York County Community Foundation
  —Heritage Funds Partnership

2006

- Jeri Jones is recipient of National Association of Geosciences Teachers "Digman" award for bringing geosciences education to the general public.
- Thirtieth anniversary of York County and York Water Company Agreement.
- Twenty-fifth anniversary of the creation of the Spring Valley Animal Activity Area.
- Twentieth anniversary of the establishment of the York County Parks Foundation Charitable Trust.

2007

- Corey King, Pennsylvania Conservation Corps, is recipient of the Golden Hammer Award for continued exemplary performance by a veteran crew leader.

2008

- Heritage Rail Trail designated by the U.S. Department of the Interior as a National Recreational Trail.
- Heritage Rail Trail selected by the National Rails-to-Trails Conservancy as a "Hall of Fame" trail as part of their National Rail Trail Network.
- Twenty York County park sites designated as part of the York County Heritage Program.
- Kudos to Corey King, recipient of the Safety Award given to Pennsylvania Conservation Corps (PCC) crew leaders for

maintaining an accident-free crew in 2008. Additionally Corey received a Certificate of Appreciation for promoting the PCC program and providing educational resources for crew leaders and corps members.

- Tom Brant recognized by *York Sunday News* as an Unsung Hero for his work at the parks department.

APPENDIX Q

Reflections of Staff and Volunteers

Two of the challenges of the 1980s were lack of funding and lack of community support for York County parks. We were fortunate to have over thirty-six hundred acres of land and some great facilities, but very few York County residents were aware that they even had a park system. In an effort to gain community support, we began providing a variety of programs, from Easter Egg hunts and concerts to more outdoor education programs; from the Treasury of Wildlife displays at Nixon Park Nature Center to day camps. Of course, our very successful Haunted Trail (eliminated in 1994) and Christmas Magic—A Festival of Lights (celebrating its twenty-fifth year in 2008) still set the system apart from most in the country.

During this time period, we had a very dedicated group of staff members and volunteers who helped make all of these activities materialize. As more people were exposed to our parks and programs, we saw increased interest and participation from the entire community. To our surprise, our budget increased as well. It was a challenging and rewarding time to be involved with the York County Park System in my home town.

— *Guy R. Walker, Parks Director, 1980–1994*

My first encounter with York County Parks occurred in the late 1970s with a Sunday afternoon nature hike at Nixon Park. I recognized the plant growing on a rock as lichen before the naturalist told us. I left that hike thrilled that science was not just in school textbooks. Afterward, I committed myself to regular visits for exercise and nature discovery.

Over the years, the unique features and special events— family reunions and picnics at Rocky Ridge, boating at William H. Kain Park, gold panning at Spring Valley—drew me to the other parks in turn. My current involvement as chair for the Friends of Wallace-Cross Mill began when area churches were asked to provide volunteer tour guides.

York County parks generate family memories, new experiences and friendships, and opportunities to learn about our wonderful world. Those who choose to volunteer in their areas of interest can become valuable and appreciated members of the park team—a winning combination!

—Judith Grove, Chair, Friends of Wallace-Cross Mill, 1999–present

"What happens to our country … depends on what we do with what others have left us." John F. Kennedy expressed this theme over and over again in his book **Profiles in Courage**. *In 1955 Senator Kennedy was referring to the American conscience, and the responsibilities of statesmen who made decisions with courage and foresight. This book brought to light the significance of individuals who assumed responsibility for future generations.*

As we turn the pages of this book, **Parks, People, Preservation, and Public Policy, we come** *to understand that we owe tremendous gratitude to those whose wisdom, contributions, and inspiration have left us with treasures in our midst. Since the early 1960s, when the "seeds of what could become …" were first planted by a small group of forward-thinking conservationists, our park system has continued to preserve our county's natural resources, provide delight for people of all ages, and most importantly, instill in each of us an appreciation for what others have granted us.*

We must remain cognizant of our role in protecting our York County Park System so that our children and our children's children can experience these treasures.

—Lori O. Mitrick, President, 2004–2007, York County Board of Commissioners

My interest in York County's parks was inspired through friendship with Charles H. Falkler, who was the Chairman of the York County Board of Parks and Recreation. In the spring of 1990, he and Guy Walker, Director of the York County Board of Parks and Recreation, asked me to meet with them.

When we met, I was advised of their interest in expanding the Nature Center at Richard M. Nixon Park to provide space to exhibit a museum-quality collection of wildlife to be donated to the county by local resident William G. Koller. To do this, it would be necessary to conduct a capital campaign. They asked me to chair what became the Treasury of Wildlife Capital Campaign, with a challenge goal of $200,000.

And so with their help, the total support of the York County Board of Commissioners, and a committee of fourteen distinguished community leaders, the challenge goal was met, and space for exhibiting Mr. Koller's animals and for an education and conference center was provided.

From the date of dedication and the permanent establishment of the York County Parks Foundation Charitable Trust, it has been my pleasure to help improve the York County parks by way of fundraising projects and to approve the accounting of same.

—Dr. Luther B. Sowers, Chair, York County Parks Foundation Charitable Trust, 1991–present

My first true involvement with the York County parks came in 1975 when we first started earnest discussions to have the York Water Company's Lake Williams, Lake Redman, and the surrounding 1,675 acres of land be used for park purposes. After nearly two years of discussions, the William H. Kain County Park was created by a fifty-year, automatically renewing agreement in which the company licenses to York County the use of its reservoir lands and waters without charge for recreational uses. We signed the agreement in late 1976, and then various federal and state agencies had to approve the arrangement. Thanks to the legal expertise of my friend and mentor, William H. Kain, supplemental agreements that solved the regulatory problems were executed by all parties and the park became a reality.

In 1984 under the leadership of Catherine I. Jones, I along with George Miller, John Buchart, Guy Walker, Samuel Conte, J. Kerr Anderson, and Floyd Jones founded the York County Parks Charitable Trust. The 501(c)(3) trust was created to assist in the development, enhancement, and operation of the parks and park facilities of York County. My involvement continues today, where I serve as a trustee and as treasurer of what is now the York County Parks Foundation Charitable Trust.

—William T. Morris, P.E., Past President & CEO,
The York Water Company
Treasurer, York County Parks Foundation Charitable Trust

Since I was a child, my happiest moments have taken place in the outdoors. Also, I love to walk to exercise. I love history, especially the Civil War era. Where could I find all those? That place would be the Heritage Rail Trail. Luckily for me, it is only five minutes from my home.

Seeing a notice in the **York Dispatch** *about the formation of a Friends of the Heritage Rail Trail Corridor (HRTC) Committee led me to the newly renovated Hanover Junction Train Station. There, I found wonderful people who shared their enthusiasm for history, railroading, and recreation on the Heritage Rail Trail, as we set about providing volunteers to the Hanover Junction Train Station and now the New Freedom Train Station. I am the chair of the Friends of the Heritage Rail Trail Corridor.*

I am most proud of my committee and their willingness to work together to make HRTC one of the best.

The people of York County and tourists from around the country and even other countries have discovered a treasure.

—Peggy Schlichter, Chair, Friends of Heritage Rail Trail Corridor, 2001–present

I became interested in the York County Parks because I utilize the parks to enjoy the many recreational activities, such as mountain biking, trail running, kayaking, and hiking.

I have been very active volunteering for trail work within the parks with an organization known as the York Area Mountain Bike Association (YAMBA). The purpose of this organization was, and continues to be, that of ensuring the longevity of the trail systems within the parks. YAMBA works in cooperation with the York County Parks to help maintain and improve the trail systems while at the same time providing education to all trail users. YAMBA not only performs general trail maintenance, but now assists the York County Parks with larger scale projects, such as trail relocations and the building of new trails.

In addition to the trail work, a few of the members of YAMBA assisted with the development of the Park Ambassadors program. Ambassadors provide information/trail ethics for trail users, advise of violations or public safety concerns, and take an active role in protecting/preserving the parks.

—Sean "Skip" Durgin, Chair, York County Advisory
Board of Parks and Recreation, 2006–present

I became interested in York County Parks when I was an educator for St. Patrick School in York in the early 1970s. I wanted to find an alternative place to take my science classes, and I had heard that Nixon Park was a wonderful location to take my junior high class.

I have been involved in York County parks for over twenty years. I served first as a volunteer in the parks working on many projects. I later was appointed to the York County Advisory Board of Parks. Following my term completion from the board, I participated in the development of the Emeritus Board of York County Parks, and I have served as the chair since its inception. When the Treasury of Wildlife project was started, I was asked to be one of the founding members. I served on that committee, and later as a trustee of the York County Parks Foundation Charitable Trust. I am also a founding member of the Gathering Leaves Society, which supports the many projects in the York County parks.

—George "Skip" Lehmann, Vice-Chair, York County
Parks Foundation Charitable Trust
Honorary Chair, York County Parks Emeritus Board,
2000–present

In the fall of 1994, York County advertised for the appointed position of County Parks Director for the York County Department of Parks and Recreation with a staff of forty. At that time, I was a product of downsizing at a local agribusiness firm, after nineteen years, and began looking for another career within the York community. I applied for the position along with 111 other applicants and was offered the position due to my past business and management experiences.

Without a clear understanding of direction, a three-year Strategic Plan was undertaken in 1996 with action steps. The four major goals identified within the first plan called for reorganization, compensation, centralization, and privatization. In 2000, a five-year Strategic Plan was completed with action steps as well. The second plan reinforced the first plan, thereby giving substance to the management and future decision-making criteria for the park system. Planning served and continues to serve as an instrumental part of this system. The planning techniques have provided numerous grant opportunities and provisions for funding.

"Government Task Forces" appointed by the County Commissioners have conducted interviews with county departments and identified their individual roles in the utilization of taxpayer dollars. One Task Force provided the following: "Overall, this committee was quite impressed by the job the parks department as well as its director is doing." Another reported that the parks department has "taken a businesslike approach in researching their customers, which probably explains the positive response from their customers."

Today, the park system continues to grow and flourish with a dedicated, professional, experienced, and passionate staff of twenty-seven, working together to provide outdoor passive recreation and leisure-time activities to the entire York community.

> *—Thomas R. Brant, Executive Director, Parks and Natural Resources Division, 1994–2009*

Did it begin by chance? No, it began at the Sylvia Newcombe Center (Pine Street School, renamed). P. Joseph Raab, President of the York County Board of Commissioners, and I, Director of Princess Center and a board member of the Girls Club of America, York, Pennsylvania, were munching on cookies and punch. He said to me, "Voni, do you realize we do not have any county parks—what are your thoughts?" I had no thoughts at that time. He suggested that we go outside and sit at the picnic table and talk about it. Discussing it for a few minutes, Joe suggested we set a date comfortable to both of us to meet in his office. We discussed how it could be accomplished. He came up with Kondor Woods.

It really became real when Joe, Mrs. Sylvia Newcombe, Executive Director, York City Parks, and I met Mr. Kondor, on site at Kondor Woods on a rainy day. The county purchased Kondor Woods comprising 750 acres of land for $150,000 dollars *and a basket of fruit from Joe Raab's farm. Kerry Flinchbaugh, William Penn Sr. High School student, eventually named the property Rocky Ridge from a naming contest.*

The York County Parks succeeded because Thomas R. Brant, Executive Director, and his administrative team had a plan— the three Ds: his direction, his desire, and his determination. However, his plan is not a plan if he does not execute it. It's obvious that he has executed his plan, because we can see the excellent results.

—Voni B. Grimes, original board member, York County Board of Parks and Recreation, 1968

After returning home from college and working a short time, I was told about a maintenance job opening at York County parks. I interviewed with the director and was hired on the spot, starting on March 19, 1989. Prior to my employment, I attended church picnics at Rocky Ridge County Park, but really was unaware of the parks department at that point.

I started as a maintenance staff person, mostly conducting trash runs twice a week, cutting grass at the Rudy Park office and doing general maintenance. In about 1985, with reorganization of the maintenance staff, I was placed on the project crew with Marvin Innerest. In the fall of 1988, I was hired as the program coordinator, which is my current title. Before I moved into my new position, Marvin and I constructed the Rudy Park Observatory through a series of donations, which eventually led to the start of the York County Astronomical Society.

What a difference forty years (or in my case, twenty-eight years) makes. What amazes me the most is the growth of the parks in both acreage and usage. This was accomplished by community leader vision, staff dedication, support from the Board of Commissioners, and support from the public.

Only four different executive directors have led the parks in my twenty-eight years. This shows how solid the parks system is and the dedication of all of the staff. I believe the support of the Board of Commissioners has been outstanding, and the communication between the executive director and board has been good. The parks have been through several budget cut periods, but have always rebounded. The popularity of the parks and the importance of having open space these days is a must.

—Jeri Jones

When I came to York County in 1965 as director of the York County Planning Commission, which at that time had been in existence for six years, there were a couple of items ongoing that related to parks and recreation. The Planning Commission had an ongoing project to map and catalogue all potential reservoir sites in the county of a certain size. My recollection is that the cutoff of the size was ten acres or more. There were two reasons for the survey. We had recently completed a Water Supply Study and Plan for the county, and there was a perceived need to look at potential water supply impoundments. The other item was Project 70, a $70-million bond issue passed by the state to be used broadly for recreational purposes. A portion of this was designated for grants to counties and municipalities for park and recreational purposes. The Planning Commission anticipated the need for parks at the county level and felt water-based recreation could be important in that regard. So that idea also related to the reservoir site inventory.

The first couple of park proposals put forth by the Planning Commission went nowhere. It remained for an election and new Board of County Commissioners to take the initiative. Joe Raab, the new President Commissioner, was a strong supporter and that board created the Board of Parks and Recreation and negotiated the purchase of the Kondor Tract that became Rocky Ridge. In the early days, the Planning Commission staff did a lot of the paperwork for the grant applications to the state and federal agencies that secured the funds for the purchase.

In the following year or year and a half, the Planning Commission provided part-time staff assistance to the Parks Board to help them get organized and get their program underway.

I remember one humorous incident during that period. Bob Hoffman had offered to donate the land that became Nixon Park. I, along with the County Commissioners and some of the Parks Board members, including Sylvia Newcombe, went over to walk the property and look things over. This included the abandoned farmhouse, which as it happened had become a meeting place or trysting spot for young folks. In a group we all walked into what was probably the living room and were stunned to see the walls covered with graffiti, including an extensive number of four-letter words. The embarrassed silence *that followed was broken by Mrs. Newcombe, who observed, "Well, at least they know how to spell."*

Of the several agencies and organizations that the Planning Commission helped form in the sixties and the seventies, none have matched or exceeded the cordiality and professional respect that has been the nature of the relationship with York County Parks.

—Reed J. Dunn Jr. aka Jack Dunn

Appendix R

York County Parks Department Contact Information

York County Department of Parks and Recreation
Administrative Headquarters
400 Mundis Race Road
York, PA 17406-9721
Phone: (717) 840-7440
Fax: (717) 840-7403
Web site: www.yorkcountyparks.org E-mail: parks@york-county.org

Bibliography

Bosselman, Fred, David Callies, and John Banta. *The Taking Issue: An Analysis of the Constitutional Limits of Land Use Control.* Washington DC: Council on Environmental Quality, 1973.

Brownson, R. C., R. A. Housemann, D. R. Brown, et al. 2000. Promoting physical activity in rural communities: walking trail access, use and effects. *American Journal of Preventive Medicine.*

Butler, George D. *Pioneers in Public Recreation.* Minneapolis, MN: Burgess, 1965.

C. S. Davidson, Inc., in cooperation with York County Board of Parks and Recreation. *Spring Valley County Park Master Plan.* September 1987. York County Government Publication. York, PA.

Cupper, Dan. *Our Priceless Heritage: Pennsylvania State Parks 1893–1993.* Commonwealth of Pennsylvania Historical and Museum Commission for Department of Environmental Resources, Bureau of State Parks, 1993.

Dunn, Diana R., ed. *County Parks: A Report of a Study of County Parks in the United States.* Washington DC: McGrath Publishing Company, 1930.

Ellis, Franklin. *History of the Susquehanna and Juniata Valleys.* Philadelphia, PA: Everts, Peck & Richards, 1886.

Environmental Design Associates, in cooperation with York County Planning Commission. *Revised Inventory: York County Park and Recreation Plan.* 1974. York, PA

The Envirothon Is Moving in 2009. Conservation Horizons. York County Conservation District, Summer-Fall 2008. York, PA.

Finding Your Home. York County Relocation Link. Genesis Publishing & Advertising, LLC. September 2007–February 2008.

Forrey, William C. *History of Pennsylvania's State Parks.* Harrisburg, PA: Bureau of State Parks, Office of Resources Management, Department of Environmental Resources, Commonwealth of Pennsylvania, 1984.

The Government of York County. York, PA: The Board of Commissioners, 2005.

Grimes, Voni B. *Bridging Troubled Waters.* York, PA: Wolf Printing, 2008.

Heritage Rail Trail County Park Development Plan. York, PA: York County Planning Commission, July 2000.

Humpel, N., A. L. Marshall, E. Leslie, et al. 2004. Changes in neighborhood walking are related to changes in perceptions of environmental attributes. *Annals of Behavioral Medicine.*

Kish/Orr and Associates and the York County Planning Commission. *Comprehensive Park and Recreation Plan for York County, PA.* April 1977. York, PA

Lemire, Robert A. *Creative Land Development: Bridge to the Future.* Lincoln, MA:, 2nd edition, 1979. Houghton Mifflin.

Loukaitou-Sideris, A. *Transportation, Land Use, and the Committee on Physical Activity, Health, Transportation and Land Use.* June 2004. Retrieved January 2008 from
McCann, Barbara. *Designing for Active Recreation.* Acti e Living Research, San Diego State University, 2005. www.trb Transportation Research Board of the National Academy of Sciences. Washington, D.C.

Minutes of the York County Board of Parks and Recreation, 1968–2009.

The Pennsylvania Heritage Parks Program. DCNR. November 1997.
Recreation and Open Space Study: A Comprehensive Plan Study. York, PA: York County Planning Commission, 1968.

Susquehanna Gorgeous: A View of History and Scenic Beauty from the Susquehanna Heritage Park. Brochure, Lancaster-York Heritage Region, 2006–2007.

Wang, G., C. A. Macera, B. Scudder-Soucie, et al. 2004. Cost effectiveness of a bicycle/pedestrian trail development in health promotion. *Preventive Medicine.*

WPA Writers' Program. Co-sponsor: Pennsylvania Historical Commission and the University of Pennsylvania. *Pennsylvania: A Guide to the Keystone State.* New York: Oxford University Press, 1940.

York County Comprehensive Plan: York County, PA. York, PA: York County Planning Commission, 1992.

York County Land Use Plan. York, PA: York County Planning Commission, 1972.

York County Open Space & Greenways Plan: A Component of the York County Comprehensive Plan. York, PA: York County Planning Commission, December 2006.

Endnotes

1   *The Mariposa Indian War, 1850–1851: Diaries of Robert Eccleston: The California Gold Rush, Yosemite and the High Sierra* by C. Gregory Crampton. University of Utah press. Special edition 1957

2   Haines, Aubrey L., *Yellowstone National Park: Its Exploration and Establishment* (Washington: United States Department of the Interior, 1974). The Yellowstone bill was introduced in Congress in January 1872; and despite a few challenges, Dawes, the author, was able to keep the bill alive. His most serious challenge came when other senators questioned how the proposed park boundaries would influence a recently designated Sioux reservation. The debate intensified, but Dawes confirmed the nation's right to claim that land when he replied, "All the treaties made by this commission are simple matters of legislation," suggesting that Congress redraw the reservation boundaries to accommodate influential men like Cooke and colleague Senator Kelly, who had significant financial interests at stake.

3   In *My First Summer in the Sierra*, Muir writes admiringly of the vague Indian "instinct" of "walking unseen": "All Indians seem to have learned this wonderful way of walking unseen, making themselves invisible." Penguin Nature Classic Series. 1987.

4   *Breaking New Ground*, Washington, D.C. Island Press, 1998, page 505. Muir's friend Theodore Roosevelt was elevated to the presidency following the assassination of President McKinley. The management of the forest reserves was transferred from the Department of the Interior to the Department of Agriculture and the new Forest Service in 1905. The chief, or forester, of the Forest Service was Gifford Pinchot. Pinchot, with Roosevelt's willing approval, restructured and professionalized the management of the national forests, as well as greatly increasing their area

and number. He had a strong hand in guiding the fledgling organization toward the utilitarian philosophy of the "greatest good for the greatest number." Pinchot added to the phrase "in the long run."

5 *York Daily Record,* http://ydr.com/news/main/February 19, 1998, by Karen M. Pihl. Pinchot originally dreamed that each of Pennsylvania's sixty-seven counties would have a conservation society of its own. "As far as we know, we are the last remaining one," said Garry Lehman, the York County society's executive secretary and past president.

6 Conversations with Raab by the author over time.

7 Video interview with Dunn by the author in 2007.

8 Interview with Stacia Hoffman Grove, daughter of Izaak Walton caretaker and friend of Stinger, by the author in 2007.

9 Based on author's conversations with McLaughlin from 1955 until his death.

10 Video interview with Luckenbaugh by the author in 2007.

11 Video interview with Newcombe by the author in 1981.

12 Video interview with Anderson by the author in 2007.

13 Conversations with Wiegand by the author from 1965 until his death.

14 Video interview with Grimes by the author in 2007.

15 Video interview with Hunt by the author in 2007.

16 York County Board of Parks and Recreation minutes April 1968.

17 York County Board of Parks and Recreation minutes April 1968.

18 Apollo 6, April 4, 1968, Launch Vehicle: Saturn V. Duration: 10 hours, 22 min, 59 seconds. The second launch of a Saturn V, overall, was not considered a success by NASA planners. During the firing of the first-stage F-1 engines, there were severe oscillations resembling the bounce of a pogo stick. Then, two second-stage J-2 engines shut down prematurely.

Later, after Apollo 6 reached orbit, the third stage J-2 engine failed to reignite for a simulated "translunar injection." Controllers decided to use the spacecraft's Service Propulsion System (SPS) engine in its place. The SPS engine burn sent the spacecraft to an altitude of 13,769 miles (22,209 kilometers). Apollo 6 pointed out the need for several "fixes" before humans could fly on the Saturn V. Source:.National Aeronautics and Space Administration

Chariots for Apollo: A History of Manned Lunar Spacecraft By Courtney G Brooks, James M. Grimwood, Loyd S. Swenson Published as NASA Special Publication-4205 in the NASA History Series, 1979.

19   National Climatic Data Center. http://weather-warehouse.com

20   Gifford Pinchot State Park, a 2,338-acre full-service park, is in northern York County along PA 177 between the towns of Rossville and Lewisberry. The park consists of reverting farm fields and wooded hillsides, with the 340-acre Pinchot Lake serving as a prime attraction. Call toll-free 888-PA-PARKS, 7 a.m. to 5 p.m. Monday to Saturday, for state park information and reservations.

21   Pennsylvania Department of Conservation and Natural Resources Web site at http://www.dcnr.state.pa.us/legal/majorlaws.aspx, Project 70 Land Acquisition and Borrowing Act, act of June 22, 1964 (Sp.Ses., P.L. 131, No. 8), 72 P.S. §§ 3946.1-3946.22. This law implements Article VIII, Section 15, of the Pennsylvania Constitution, which provides that "the Commonwealth may be authorized by law to create debt and to issue bonds to the amount of $70,000,000 for the acquisition of land for State parks, reservoirs and other conservation and recreation and historical preservation purposes, and for participation by the Commonwealth with political subdivisions in the acquisition of land for parks, reservoirs and other conservation and recreation and historical preservation purposes, subject to such conditions and limitations as the General Assembly may prescribe." The act authorizes the Commonwealth and political subdivisions to acquire suitable lands by eminent domain. Under the act, no lands acquired pursuant to the act may be disposed of or used for purposes other than for recreation, conservation, and historical purposes without the express approval of the General Assembly.

22   Maurice Rotival: French planning on a world-scale (Part II) by C. Hein in *Planning Perspectives* 17(4) 1 October 22, pp. 325–344 (20) ,

published by Routledge, part of the Taylor & Francis Group.

23   The Lee Anderson Papers, consisting of nearly five thousand items, are housed in the Washington University Library. Many of them were composed during Lee Anderson's residency in Potosi, now Spring Valley Park.

24   York County Comprehensive Plan.

25   Secretary of the Interior Stewart L. Udall's memorandum of January 15, 1969, to the director of the National Park Service. This communication was sent five days before Udall's term expired. The incoming director, Walter Hickel of Alaska, was promoting a plan to "use" the parks for revenue—oil, timber, etc. Udall reiterated his management principles, concluding with the admonition, "What we have added, basically, in the last four and one-half years, is the realization that if we do not inculcate in the American people a determination to preserve and restore a quality environment, then all of the National Park values, which are an indivisible part of the total environment, will slowly erode and eventually disappear."

26   The National Park Service assists communities interested in attaining the Federal NHA designation by helping them craft a regional vision for heritage preservation and development. The agency also provides a variety of types of assistance to areas once designated—administrative, financial, policy, technical, and public information. The NPS seeks to serve as a catalyst by offering assistance to designated heritage areas only for a limited number of years. (While the legislation creating a heritage area limits federal financial support to no more than fifteen years under the assumption that the area would become financially self-sufficient, in fact, every area that has reached the fifteen-year mark has requested a continuation of taxpayer support and the Congress has extended it.)
October 23, 2007

National Heritage Areas: Costly Economic Development Schemes that Threaten Property Rights
by Cheryl Chumley and Ronald D. Utt, Ph.D.
Backgrounder #2080 The Heritage Foundation

27   Watt's tenure as Secretary of the Interior was marked by controversy, stemming primarily from his alleged hostility to environmentalism and

support of the development and use of federal lands by foresting, ranching, and other commercial interests. He advocated that eighty million acres of undeveloped land in the United States be opened for drilling and mining in the year 2000. *Time Magazine*, 24 October, 1983.

28 *Sunday Patriot News,* April 26, 1981, p. 2, Harry McLaughlin.

29 CNN, U.S. Briefs, March 12, 1996.

30 *1966 York County Pennsylvania Recreation & Open Space Comprehensive Plan Study*, York County Planning Department, Reed J. Dunn Jr., Director.

31 *York Daily Record*, March 7, 1975, "County golf course eyed for $500,000."

32 Board minutes throughout 1981 document the incidents.

33 See Gathering Leaves Society, Appendix K.

34 Conversation with the author in 1976.

35 Fitz, a preeminent manufacturer of waterwheels, was located in Hanover, PA, until the late twentieth century, making restoration of the Fitz wheel a significant contribution.

36 Money given to York County at the time would have gone into the General Fund. When the York County Charitable Trust came into existence, it made it possible to give directly to the parks department for special intentions.

37 Rails to Trails Conservancy president David Burwell, "2000 miles of US rails were abandoned a year in 1998," *PR Newswire*, October 19, 1998.

38 *York Dispatch*, 19 October, 1993, Letters to the Editor.

39 A passive recreation area refers to a mix of uses in a neighborhood park, undeveloped land, or minimally improved lands, which include the following: landscaped area, natural area, ornamental garden, nonlandscaped greenspace, stairway, decorative fountain, picnic area, water body, or trail without recreational staffing. Active Living Research,

San Diego University, 3900 Fifth Avenue, Suite 310, San Diego, CA 92103, www.activelivingresearch.org.

Passive Recreation Area Law & Legal Definition. A passive recreation area is generally an undeveloped space or environmentally sensitive area that requires minimal development. Entities such as a parks department may maintain passive recreation areas for the health and well-being of the public and for the preservation of wildlife and the environment. The quality of the environment and "naturalness" of an area is the focus of the recreational experience in a passive recreation area. Passive recreation may be defined as a nonmotorized activity that: offers constructive, restorative, and pleasurable human benefits and fosters appreciation and understanding of open space and its purpose; is compatible with other passive recreation uses; does not significantly impact natural, cultural, scientific, or agricultural values; requires only minimal visitor facilities and services directly related to safety to minimize the impact Passive Recreation Area Law& Legal Definition found on USLegal.com.

40   See Income chart in Appendix C.

41   Independent Sector, *The Value of Volunteer Time*, http://www. independentsector.org.

42   Community volunteer hours, 32,324; Pennsylvania Conservation Corps employment skills training for youth, 10,400 hours; 7 interns and parks practicum students, 1520 hours.

43   Letter from Denise M. Smith, a resident of Lower Windsor Township interested in land preservation,

RD 12 Box 237 Gun Club Road York, Pa
September 1991

To:York County Parks Board
    600 Mundis Race Road
    York, PA

Dear Mr. Guy Walker:

My name is Denise Smith and I am a citizen interested in land reservation, living in Lover Windsor Township, a rural community in York, Pennsylvania. York County is one of the most scenic areas and contains some of the most fertile farmland in the Commonwealth. Unfortunately it is rapidly being gobbled up by development. Within this small township is a parcel of property known as the Lauxmont Farms. This spectacular piece of property that has been in *National Geographic* in March 1985 is in jeopardy of being developed.

We have begun a citizens group interested in preserving this valuable and historic property. Our group began with just six to eight individuals and has grown significantly. We have tried to raise some monies to help with expenses and have written many people. And made many phone calls trying to inform people of more influential nature of our concern. We have circulated petitions in the hopes of educating people as to the importance of this piece of property and we're hoping the two thousand plus signatures on the petions will positively influence the individuals that are responsible for making the final decisions concerning this fragile area.

The American Farmland Trust and other organizations are aware of the property and its importance and have formed a coalition to protect the land. The York Count Farmland Trust, our local private organization, which is only one year old, is working diligently to help AFT in any way that they can. We are all aware of the fact that our citizens group nor the York County Farmland Trust can do much financially to help the situation because of the magnitude, but we are offering our support in any way that we can. Attached are fact sheets prepared by the Executive Director of the York County Farmland Trust to provide pertinent information about the property.

As the spokesperson for People for the Preservation of Lauxmont Farms, I am asking you for your support. I have no way of knowing how or in what way your organization can help, but we do seek your support. Obviously, much financial support is needed to secure the easements on the property. These easements placed on the property would insure that the property forever remain farmland or open space. We know that you share our concern for the future of these unique areas of beauty.

A letter of intent or of financial commitment would be greatly appreciated. Any other guidance you can offer would obviously help. I thank you in advance for the support I know that I can count on from you, another organization that is concerned that these areas will be lost forever.

Sincerely,
Denise M. Smith

Enclosure
Lauxmont Farm Information Sheet
August 1991

So as to dispel any rumors regarding the Lauxmont Farm Project, the following information sheet has been prepared and distributed to all YCFT Board Members.

The information contained herein, has been verified with the court appointed trustee and the other coalition organizations. The following is to date and accurate, 15 August 1991.

The American Farmland Trust, and other regional and national conservation organizations together with assistance from the York County Farmland Trust are attempting to secure agricultural easement on the property at Lauxmont Farm, in Lower Windsor Township, to assure that the land is preserved as productive agricultural land and open space in perpetuity.

Preservations efforts have been aimed at permanent protection of most, if not all of the 1392 acres. However, a more realistic scenario appears to have protection efforts by various organizations identified with those portions of the property most closely aligned with the organizations missions statements. Meaning—both AFT and YCFT are concentrating on those that are the most appropriate for agricultural uses. These lands have been identified by topography and soils, as those lying to the southern end of the property. This area consists of about 650-700 acres.

Due to the bankruptcy status on this property, all transactions involving property sales, placing of conservation easements, timber removal, crop proceeds, etc., are and must be approved through the court trustee. Lee Haller (court-appointed trustee) has been allowing the Kohrs to receive certain monies from crops, breeding and rentals directly, acknowledging that there are certain general living expenses and bills that need to be paid.

The "timber cut" referred to at YCFTs August Board meeting, as indicated at the board meeting, is to be a selective cut. This has been approved by Lee Haller, the proceeds are to pay for insurance and other expenses. Mr. Haller felt that the two hundred trees to be cut were in an area where there would be no damage to the value of the property and is considered to be "normal course." He assured me that "all is in order" and the "the Kohrs have no desire to diminish the value of their property, particularly given the fact that the property or at least a good portion of it will need to be sold." To my understanding any transactions involving the land must be cleared with Mr. Haller—even certain entries onto the property.

The American Farmland Trust has authorized Dr. Robert Barr to perform a market analysis and appraisal on the Lauxmont Farm. The appraisal is to be completed by the first week in September—until that time there is no clear understanding of exactly what the property is "worth" in today's market. After the appraisal is completed, AFT will be presenting the finding to their board of directors at the September meeting.

The general feeling from Bob Wagner and Lee Haller, is that the preservation effort right now has a "wonderful chance to come together if orchestrated well …" Lee mentioned that he has promised to wait for the proposal from AFT, although there is a developer from Philadelphia who has proposal for the entire property and is ready to move. The development plan would take about ten years to complete—and Haller knows this is not popular, but his job is to move the property.

The property is currently in Chapter 11 (not Chapter 7) which allows for reorganization. Therefore, any efforts made by the Kohrs to hold on to some of their property is perfectly allowable. although the trustee did mention that he is currently entertaining any and all offers, and if the money is right … there would be little that the Kohrs could do to arrest outright sale.

The efforts of the American Farmland Trust and other coalition organizations is to protect the land. This is not an effort to "bail-out" anyone. nor is it an effort to displace anyone. The priorities lie in the attributes of seeing this spectacular piece of property perpetually protected.

GENERAL STATISTICS AND INFORMATION
Six total tracts currently comprise the Lauxmont Farm, they range in size from 59 to 881 acres.

Approximately 830 acres is Class I-IV soils classified by SCS (60%) remaining 560 acres Class V-VII

Historic Significance: Byrd Leibhart Site – largest Susquehannock Indian fort along river. Misc. Indian artifacts excavated from property at York County Historic Society & Museum in Harrisburg. Upwards of 500 Indian burial sites. Estimates of first inhabitants circa. 3000-6000 BC. Area once considered for the siting of the nation's capital.

Over ten miles of road wrap throughout the scenic hills of the property, thirteen homes ranging from circa. 1760s to early 1900s (not all inhabited). Private Japanese rock garden at main house.

Tidbits: Famous persons who have visited—John Wayne, Kate Smith, Col. Nimitz, FDR etc.

The farm and the area surrounding it are well known to York County residents for its beauty, history, and value to the community as both a farm and an open space. The York County Farmland Trust is working to build a coalition of support for the preservation effort among area residents, businesses, and any other interested organizations. If development of all of these properties were to occur at Lauxmont, the impact on the environment in the Wrightsville community would be profound. Below are only a few of the dramatic impacts which may occur with development of Lauxmont Farms on the quality of life in Wrightsville and surrounding townships.

Area residents' taxes will increase rapidly. New development will spur needs for infrastructure, infrastructure maintenance, water and sewer projects, increased fire and police protection and an array of services that are otherwise unnecessary.

Environmental impacts such as increased soil erosion and need for storm water management; loss of wildlife habitat; increased source generation of chemical pollution; increases in contaminating emissions from automobiles, homes and commercial establishments; and a loss of groundwater recharge potential.

There will be a substantial increase in traffic, congestion, and noise.

The valuable open space quality of the Lauxmont Farm will be lost forever. Lauxmont is famous for its beautiful green rolling hills and panoramic views of the Susquehanna River. Development which is not sensitive to the fragility of the land and the view sheds will negatively affect this quality forever.

44   See list of parks awards in Appendix P.

INDEX